SOU
AFRICA

Martin Gostelow
and
Bernard Joliat

JPMGUIDES

Contents

This Way South Africa

Land of Treasures

With as many facets as a kaleidoscope, the land now called the Republic of South Africa has been attracting Europeans since the second half of the 17th century. Its strategic importance, fertile soils, enviable climate, fabulous mineral riches and unparalleled natural attractions have long been irresistible lures.

At the tip of the African continent, between the Atlantic and Indian oceans, South Africa has a varied landscape. The craggy mountains of the Drakensberg could hardly be more different from the red plains of the Kalahari, the forests and lakes of the Garden Route, or the acacia bush of the Kruger Park. Molten gold being poured in the mines of bustling Johannesburg provides a striking counterpoint to the Stone Age rock art, traditional Zulu villages and sleepy settler towns studded with Cape Dutch buildings found elsewhere in the country.

For years, the political policies of the apartheid era ensured that the majority of potential international visitors shunned South Africa as a holiday destination. All that has changed since 1994, when the first democratic election was held: today, South Africa ranks as the most popular tourist destination on the continent.

Towns, Flowers and Vineyards

A busy commercial city, Johannesburg offers the sort of sights you might expect in Manhattan. In its pagan temples of concrete and smoked glass, the sacred rites are centred on the fluctuating prices of gold, platinum, uranium and diamonds. Looking out over its sprawling suburbs after a lengthy flight, you'll find it difficult to believe that Johannesburg has only just celebrated its first century of existence.

The region around Pretoria—called Jacaranda City for its avenues of trees that blossom into purple clouds in October—is scattered with mansions and monuments that encapsulate in stone and bronze the country's exciting history.

Cape Town, beautifully sited beneath Table Mountain, forms with the Cape Peninsula a floral kingdom. South of the city, a botanical garden displays half of the 18,000 flower species found within the Republic.

Travelling inland from Cape Town, you pass through some of 3

A GEOGRAPHY LESSON

Covering more than five times the area of the British Isles, South Africa is a melting pot of the human race. On territory measuring 1,221,037 sq km (476 968 sq miles), a population made up of 30 million blacks, 5 million whites (58% Afrikaners and 39% of English tongue), 3.4 million people of mixed race and 1 million Asians are now endeavouring to build one of the richest countries on earth.

the lushest land on earth. The vineyards of Stellenbosch, Paarl and Franschhoek produce some of South Africa's best-known wines. Those who choose to follow the Garden Route along the south coast can make stops at a dozen beach resorts as well as taking a look at industrial Port Elizabeth and East London—not forgetting the inland detour to the ostrich farms of Oudtshoorn.

Flanked by extensive beaches of fine sand, Durban, with its sophisticated lifestyle and facilities for water sports, makes a splendid starting point or finale to a tour along the shores of the Indian Ocean. To the west stand the towers and crags of the Drakensberg, a mountain wall to be crossed before you reach the rich, rolling farmlands of the Free State.

Fascinating Cultures

Wearing headdresses made from buffalo horn, their bodies daubed with war paint and hung with tribal ornaments, the descendants of the mighty *impis* (armies) of Shaka Zulu wait in ambush, leaping suddenly out of the Zululand landscape to catch visitors unawares. Such historically evocative encounters—friendly nowadays—give the actors the chance to earn a rand or two, and are a delight for the photographer.

Other cultures also enjoy the opportunity to explain their traditions and astonish visitors with their rites, costumes, colours and art. The most surprising of these are the Ndebele, a minority community in the Pretoria region. Long before western Cubists dreamed up the idea, Ndebele artists were practising this type of painting, covering the walls of their dwellings in radiant colours and bold geometrical patterns.

Safari Country

South Africa is the domain of the wild animal—close encounters are virtually guaranteed. Hluhluwe, Umfolozi, Mala Mala, Londolozi and Sabi Sabi, among many other national and private game reserves, offer you the privilege of seeing the great beasts in their own environment—rhinoceros, elephant, hippopotamus, lion, leopard, cheetah, buffalo, giraffe, antelope and zebra are all here. However, none of these reserves can compare in scale or variety with the Kruger National Park, South Africa's greatest animal sanctuary.

Listen to the Sunrise

In South Africa, everything is possible. Have you ever dreamed of travelling the streets of Durban in a rickshaw pulled by a Zulu warrior dressed in full tribal regalia? Can you conjure up the atmosphere of a Mzoumba tribal dance, where a hundred drums beat in rhythm and a thousand feet hammer the ground? Have you ever listened to the sounds of sunrise or dusk over the African bush? One thing is certain: however long your stay in this country, it won't be long enough to sample all the attractions.

Where to Stay

You'll be pleasantly surprised by the choice and high standards of accommodation and hospitality. At the top end are five-star hotels, especially in the Cape Town area and the prosperous suburbs of Johannesburg. The coastal resorts near Durban and along the Garden Route have hotels for every budget. Along the well-trodden holiday routes, in the Drakensberg mountains, the Northern and Western Cape, Mpumalanga, the Northern Province and the Free State, country-house hotels and family homes offering bed and breakfast are ready to welcome you. In the game parks, the options include self-catering in well-equipped chalets, the hotels near major park entrances and the ultimate in luxury at one of the private lodges.

Early Times

Africa is the cradle of humanity. The East African Rift Valley has yielded fossils that represent practically every stage in hominid evolution. South Africa's oldest-known hominid fossil skull, discovered in the Sterkfontein caves near Johannesburg, has been dated to 2$\frac{1}{2}$ million years ago.

The earliest inhabitants of southern Africa were hunter-gatherers. This lifestyle was still practised in arid and mountainous parts of the region by the San (or Bushmen) in the 15th century, when Europeans first landed at the Cape. In more moist areas, hunter-gatherers had been all but supplanted by pastoralists such as the Khoikhoi (or Hottentots) of the southern Cape and Bantu of the eastern coastline and interior.

The First Europeans

In 1485, with the arrival of Diego Cão, the Portuguese became the first recorded Europeans to set foot on the soil of southern Africa. The following year, on December 8, 1486, Bartolomeu Dias landed at the place now known as Mossel Bay. A few weeks later he discovered the site of the future Cape Town. Ten years on, Vasco da Gama sailed from the bay of Saint Helena to the coast of Natal. He was the first man in history to round the Cape of Good Hope and open the route to India for western navigators.

Early Settlers

The "European" history of South Africa had begun, but no one thought of settling in the region until 1652. Commanding three ships and some hundred men, Jan Van Riebeeck established a strategic revictualling point at the Cape for the ships of the Dutch East India Company. Five years later the first colonists had arrived, and in 1685, 200 Huguenots, French Protestant refugees, landed near the Cape, where they soon integrated with the established Dutch community. They also had the foresight to introduce the cultivation of vines. Dutch, French and, later, German settlers gradually began to think of themselves as one people, the Afrikaners, speaking a form of Dutch called Afrikaans.

Boers against Bantus

Next to settle were Malays and Malagasy, brought in by the Dutch East India Company which needed the labour. Some colonists who found it hard to bear the con-

San engravings at Riemvasmaak in the Northern Cape depict animal, human and geometric forms.

straints imposed by the Company ventured to the east and the north, becoming semi-nomadic pastoral farmers known as the *trekboeren*. Weakened by smallpox and other diseases, the Khoikhoi were unable to resist this expansion, although some intermarried with others of the Cape population. Today their descendants form part of the mixed race Cape Coloured community.

The Bantus, especially the Xhosas of the eastern Cape and the Zulus who were firmly settled on the fertile plains of Natal, were a different matter. The first of the frontier wars between Boers and Bantus took place in 1779.

Prosperity

The Cape began to prosper, largely through trade with the *trekboeren* who bartered their cattle for arms, coffee and sugar. Rivalry between England and France (which was allied with the Dutch), both in the Americas and in Europe, had its repercussions in South Africa. The British, who wanted to control the route to the Indies, captured the Cape in 1795 but returned it to the Batavian Republic, as the Dutch government was then called, under the Treaty of Amiens in 1802. (By that time the Dutch East Indian Company was extinct.) But the eastern districts were in turmoil, 7 and with the resumption of the Napoleonic Wars, the British recaptured the Cape from Napoleon's Dutch allies in 1806. Their title was confirmed in 1814 by the Treaty of Paris.

The British Arrive

British colonization did not begin in earnest until 1820, with the arrival of 5000 settlers in what is today the Eastern Cape. With them they brought notions of freedom of the press, civil rights and humanitarian ideals. They established Anglican missions and English as the official language. In 1828 the Khoikhoi and Cape Coloured people were given freedom of movement; slavery was abolished in 1834. The emancipated slaves and the Khoikhoi became a rural and urban working class. All these measures were unacceptable to the Boers, who were also forced to return to the Bantus land acquired in the frontier wars of 1834–35.

The Boers Leave

Many Afrikaners came to the conclusion that they could not live as they wished under British rule. Between 1835 and 1843, some 12,000 of them, together with their cattle, sheep and wagons, set out, Bible in hand, on the Great Trek. Some settled by the Orange River, others continued northwards to the Limpopo and the future Transvaal, the remainder travelled eastwards across the Drakensberg mountains and into Natal. Many were killed by Zulu and Matabele warriors, but the decisive victory over the Zulus came at Blood River in 1838. It enabled most of the Voortrekkers to stake out farms in Natal. The hero of the day was General Andries Pretorius, to whom the city of Pretoria owes its name.

British-Boer Rivalry

The trekkers founded two new republics based on strict, puritanical Calvinism: the Transvaal in 1852 and the Orange Free State in 1854. South Africa was thus divided into two camps—the Afrikaner republics and the British colonies, where in the course of time a relatively liberal tradition developed.

With the intention of unifying the four white states of southern Africa (the Cape, Natal, Orange Free State and the Transvaal), the British annexed the Transvaal in 1877. They then moved to eliminate the danger presented by the Zulus' military strength. Under their chief Cetshwayo, the Zulus routed a large British force at Isandhlwana in 1879 but were conquered the following year at Ulundi. The Transvaal Afrikaners, who had initially accepted annexation, eventually put up a formidable resistance led by Paul

Kruger, Marthinus Pretorius (son of Andries) and Piet Joubert. The struggle ended with the defeat of a British force at Majuba Hill in 1881. The Transvaal thereby gained full internal autonomy despite nominal British control.

Gold and Diamonds

The discovery of diamonds at Kimberley in 1867 and of the Witwatersrand goldfields in 1886 attracted a tidal wave of prospectors and opportunists from many countries, most of them British subjects. In the Transvaal, Kruger denied these *Uitlanders* (foreigners) civil rights, but they continued to pour in. By 1896 they outnumbered the Boers seven to one.

Meanwhile, in the Cape, Cecil Rhodes, diamond magnate and controller of De Beers, had appeared on the scene. As prime minister he formed an alliance with the Afrikaner Hofmeyr which held the hope of healing the Anglo-Afrikaner rift and of building good relations between whites and non-whites in the Cape colony. But as the European race to colonize Africa accelerated, Rhodes began annexing territory surrounding the Afrikaner republics and making plans for a British South African federation.

You can go down the mine shaft at Gold Reef City, now a museum.

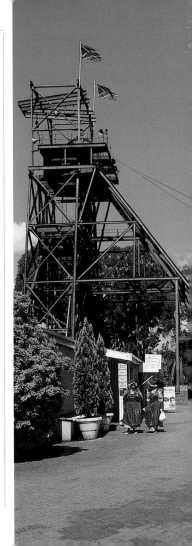

Frustrated by Kruger, Rhodes plotted his overthrow. At the end of 1895, one of his supporters, Dr Jameson, led a raid into the Transvaal, ostensibly to "save" the Uitlanders from persecution. But they failed to rise as Jameson had hoped. He was forced to surrender, and Rhodes resigned as prime minister. When the British presented Kruger with an ultimatum on the Uitlanders' franchise, war was inevitable. Kruger remained unmoved, and in 1899 the second Anglo-Boer war broke out.

The Boer War

Although they sympathized with Kruger's cause, the Boer community in the Cape did not rise up but offered only moral support. Both sides paid a heavy price in a war that was to last three years. At first the Boers held the British forces at bay at the Tugela in Natal for almost a year while laying siege to Ladysmith, Mafeking (now Mafikeng) and Kimberley. Once the British had broken through at Tugela and invaded the Orange Free State, the Boers began to use guerrilla tactics against their columns. By 1902, the British were burning Boer farms and interning civilians in camps where more than 20,000 died—the first "concentration camps". The Boers appealed for help, and many volunteers responded—Irish, American, even Russian—seeing the anti-colonialist cause as their own. But any hopes of support from the governments of Germany, France and the Netherlands were dashed. Britain called on its generals, Roberts and Kitchener, together with troops from Australia, New Zealand and Canada, as well as 100,000 black and Cape Coloured auxiliaries. The Boers were eventually forced to surrender. Kruger signed the Treaty of Vereeniging in the Transvaal on May 31, 1902. The British were left in charge of the goldfields, but their losses totalled more than 25,000 men.

The Start of Segregation

Amnesty was granted to the rebels, along with freedom for prisoners, recognition of the Afrikaner language and financial help with reconstruction. Four years later, the two erstwhile warring communities came together to suppress the revolt of the Zulus of Natal. The Union of South Africa was declared on May 31, 1910, with the Boer General Louis Botha as Prime Minister. This was two years before the foundation of the African National Congress (ANC) which aspired to persuade the white community to accord blacks full political rights. It proved to be a vain hope, and in 1913 the Native Land Act prevented Africans from acquiring land outside the reserves.

With the Allies

The economic crisis of 1929 and the outbreak of World War II in 1939 accentuated the division between the English and Afrikaner communities. Pro-German in the great European conflict, the Afrikaners tried to keep their country neutral. But prime minister Jan Smuts, who had little sympathy with Nazi ideals, brought South Africa into the war on the side of the Allies. Nevertheless, a party of 400,000 Nazi enthusiasts, South Africa's Ossewabrandwag, openly supported Hitler.

Farewell to the Commonwealth

Protests and strikes by the black trade unions from 1940 onwards met with repression, especially after the election, in 1948, of an ultra-right-wing Nationalist government under D. F. Malan. In 1950, mixed marriages or even sexual relations between black and white were prohibited, as well as any political party or association opposed to apartheid (the Afrikaans word for "separateness"). In 1952, the work permit became obligatory for black Africans, and the passbook was required for any travelling. A demonstration at Sharpeville on March 21, 1960 by the ANC movement was fired on by security forces, killing 61 blacks. The ANC, directed first by Albert Luthuli (Nobel laureate for peace in 1960) and later by Nelson Mandela, was outlawed. Following a referendum, the Union of South Africa withdrew from the Commonwealth and became the Republic of South Africa.

Set-back

The politics of apartheid were pursued despite general worldwide condemnation. To limit the danger threatened by the overcrowded townships, some of the black population was moved out to "homelands", conceived to encourage "separate development". In this way the artificial states of Transkei, Ciskei, Bophuthatswana and Venda were created, though they were refused recognition by the UN. Excluded from international sport and the object of commercial boycotts, South Africa suffered more and more from its isolation.

Revolution

A new law that obliged all schools to use the Afrikaans language in their teaching provoked the Soweto riots of 1976. The incidents marked the beginning of an undercover revolution. Pieter Botha, elected President in 1978, tried in vain to save apartheid by easing its laws superficially, largely under pressure from local financial interests who were concerned by the export of capital. 11

The Constitution of 1983 attempted to increase the power of the Indian and mixed race populations. In 1986 the laws against mixed marriages and interracial relations were dropped, the passbook was suppressed, and certain facilities were granted to black leaders.

The Search for Peace

Desmond Tutu, the Anglican archbishop of Cape Town, exerted his influence to achieve better understanding and mutual respect between the opposing groups; he received the 1984 Nobel Peace Prize for his efforts. However, the violence continued with the support of the ANC, whose leaders, including Nelson Mandela, had been arrested and condemned to life imprisonment in 1964. Those who escaped arrest were forced into exile. A state of emergency was declared in 1985 and continued until 1990.

The End of Apartheid

In 1989, Frederik De Klerk was elected by the National Party to succeed Pieter Botha. At his investiture, De Klerk promised freedom to all political prisoners and lifted the ban on the ANC and other dissident groups. He later released Nelson Mandela, who had spent 27 years behind bars. The two men launched an anti-apartheid policy together,

challenged by the far-right AWB party led by the notorious Eugene Terreblanche.

At the end of 1991, the Convention for Democratic South Africa (Codesa) was created by 17 parties, who established the basis for a new united South Africa free of racial discrimination. Only the extreme left and the extreme right abstained.

The Triumph of Reason

In a referendum held the following year, 68 per cent of the white population accepted the movement towards reform. The opponents of De Klerk and Mandela, in particular the Zulu Inkatha movement and white conservatives, then entered the fray and played their last cards. The country was on the brink of civil war, but reason prevailed and the first multiracial elections were programmed for 1994. The UN lifted its economic sanctions, Frederik De Klerk and Nelson Mandela jointly received the Nobel Peace Prize, and South Africa rejoined the Commonwealth.

Modern Times

Multi-racial classes started the school year in 1994. On Sunday, April 24, 1994, long queues of people of all races and all cultures formed in front of the polling stations to exercise their right to vote. To general surprise and relief, the elections passed off peacefully and Nelson Mandela was elected President, the first black to govern South Africa. Due largely to his wisdom, the country's peaceful transition to a majority rule was a political miracle. Now a younger generation of leaders headed by Thabo Mbeki (elected in 1999) work new wonders, having to deal with an array of long-simmering problems: a shortage of low-cost housing, mass unemployment, alarming levels of crime and an AIDS epidemic. Tourism is a bright spot, a major earner and creator of jobs. Combined with the South Africans' natural hospitality, this means you'll be made more than welcome.

NELSON MANDELA

South Africa's first democratically elected president, Nelson Rohlihlahla Mandela was born on July 18, 1918 in the village of Qunu near Umtata in the Transkei. While studying law in Johannesburg in 1941, Mandela became involved in the African National Congress (ANC), the organization founded in 1912 to campaign for full citizenship for all South Africans.

Non-violent acts of defiance against the apartheid regime led to Mandela's arrest on a charge of high treason in 1956, but after five years of legal wrangling, the case was dismissed. He then went "underground", making illegal trips abroad and promoting a programme of strikes and sabotage. But the ANC was ill prepared for this role. It had been penetrated by the state security forces and in August 1962 Mandela was arrested again and sentenced first to five years, and then to life imprisonment.

Robben Island, within sight of Cape Town, became his home for almost 20 years. In winter rain and summer heat, the convicts chipped the white rock in its quarry; Mandela's eyesight was damaged by the dazzling reflection and dust. But the world had not forgotten. He became its most celebrated political prisoner and when apartheid at last began to crumble, there was no alternative open to the government but to talk to him. He was moved to the mainland, then to a hospital, and finally released on 11 February 1990. In 1993 he and De Klerk were jointly awarded the Nobel Peace Prize.

Only Nelson Mandela's moral authority and astonishing degree of forgiveness could have held the nation together in the ensuing elections and the challenges that followed. South Africa must hope that his wisdom and vision will continue to guide his successors.

On the Scene

South Africa is a mosaic of ethnic groups and landscapes, of cultures and traditions, of wild beasts and rare plants. Each of its provinces covers an immense area offering constant variety and a wide diversity of natural and cultural sites. It is impossible to see everything in one trip, but why worry? After all, you will surely want to come back to this land of adventure.

This book follows the division of South Africa into nine provinces, adopted in 1995. These are Gauteng (previously PWV), Limpopo (formerly Northern) Province, the North-West, Mpumalanga (formerly the Eastern Transvaal), the Free State, KwaZulu/Natal, the Eastern Cape, the Northern Cape and the Western Cape.

▶ GAUTENG

Johannesburg, Soweto, Pretoria, Cullinan, Kwa-Ndebele

Gauteng—"place of gold" in the Sotho language—was delineated as recently as 1994, when the country's four established provinces (whose borders conformed to those of the pre-Union Cape and Natal Colonies and Transvaal and Free State Boer Republics) were divided into nine smaller ones. Consisting of Pretoria, the Witwatersrand, Johannesburg and

The high- and low-rises of Johannesburg's city centre.

Vereeniging, Gauteng is by far the smallest of South Africa's new provinces, but also the most urbanized and densely populated, supporting roughly 10 million people. With direct flights from many foreign cities, Johannesburg International Airport is the primary gateway to South Africa, and it also serves Pretoria and Sun City. For most visitors, however, Gauteng serves as little more than an overnight stop and springboard for travels to more scenic parts of the country.

15

Johannesburg

Situated on a plateau at an altitude of 1,800 m (5,900 ft), Johannesburg is Southern Africa's commercial and economic metropolis, and the focal point of what is certainly the largest urban conglomeration in Africa. Yet, by the standards of European cities, Johannesburg is barely out of its infancy, founded on an otherwise unremarkable tract of grassland in 1886, when one George Harrison found a huge nugget of gold and triggered off a rush that attracted thousands of hopeful prospectors. The boomtown of Johannesburg, which fell to the British at the end of the Boer War (1899–1902), grew to become one of the great cities of the world.

City Centre

Above a busy African street scene, many of the tall modern office buildings stand empty, abandoned in the flight to safer and pleasanter suburbs. The grid-iron street pattern is broken only by Diagonal Street, a metaphor for the stock exchange, whose building used to stand beside it. Erected in 1983, the nearby Anglo-American Building has the form of a diamond whose facets reflect the colours of the sky.

Some unusual souvenirs can be found in the shops of African sorcerers—magic potions, fetishes and statuettes, along with a fine selection of aphrodisiacs. Asian shopkeepers have a wide variety of Indian goods on sale at Oriental Plaza, further west in the Newtown area.

Market Theatre

Northwest of Diagonal Street, some of South Africa's best actors are to be seen performing in the four theatres of the Market Theatre complex. There are also two art galleries, a restaurant, a bar and a shopping area, not to mention a flea market every weekend—in short, something for everyone. The nearby Museum-Africa in Bree Street has a remarkable collection of Stone Age Bushman paintings.

Hillbrow

North of the city centre near Hillbrow Hospital, the Adler Museum of Medicine and Dentistry is one of Johannesburg's more disconcerting museums. Along with a collection of 19th-century medical instruments is a curious African herbarium and the medical bag of an African sorcerer. A display is devoted to Professor Christiaan Barnard, who carried out the world's first heart transplant in 1969.

Traditionally cosmopolitan, Hillbrow is today a focal point for legal and illegal migrants from elsewhere in Africa, as well as having the unenviable reputa-

Johannesburg's economic heart beats in Diagonal Street.

tion of being the single biggest crime hotspot in the country. Peppered with night clubs and restaurants, most of them decidedly disreputable, Hillbrow is—wisely—avoided by most tourists.

Built in 1896 in Tudor style, Windybrow Theatre houses the headquarters of the drama section of the Council for Theatrical Arts. Fringe-theatre productions, often very good, are staged here.

Ellis Park

At Doornfontein, 3 km (almost 2 miles) east of the city centre, Ellis Park attracts crowds of avid rugby fans. With a bit of luck, visitors may be able to watch a top-level match, recalling that this is where South Africa's Springboks won the world rugby championship in 1995, with President Nelson Mandela proudly cheering them on.

Gold Reef City

The mining town of Gold Reef City has become Johannesburg's principal tourist attraction. The headgear of Crown Mines No. 14 shaft marks the site of what was once the world's deepest mine, at 3,200 m (10,500 ft), employing 30,000 miners. It closed in 1977 and has been transformed into a vast theme park and open-air museum. Accurate historical recon- 17 structions transport visitors back in time to the 1880s and the early days of the Gold Rush. A lift takes you down an old mine shaft to a depth of 220 m (720 ft). Above ground, the saloons, banks and shops of the era recreate the old-time atmosphere. The programme of attractions includes a twice-daily performance of African dances by the Gumboot Dancers, clad in the miners' standard issue rubber boots.

Northern Suburbs

Over the past decade or so, big business and upmarket commercial interests (including most tourist facilities) have generally migrated from the city centre to the leafy northern suburbs. The prestigious suburb of Sandton—a separate municipal entity—is the site of the largest concentration of tourist hotels around Johannesburg, as well as several large shopping malls.

Also serviced by several classy hotels and shops, Rosebank is of interest for its Rooftop Market, an excellent place to go curio shopping. By contrast, the trendy suburb of Melville is studded with lively street cafés, live music venues, arty shops and individualistic restaurants.

Soweto

From 1945 onwards, the urbanization of the blacks intensified, bringing about serious problems of health and hygiene with the appearance of shanty towns. Disease, delinquency and prostitution were added to the difficulties of assimilation. To control the

---

SOWETO SIGHTS

From Johannesburg or Pretoria, private operators will take you on a tour of South Africa's most famous township. Small groups of visitors are guided by formidable local ladies, who point out the locations that made the news during the anti-apartheid campaigns: Regina Mundi Church, focus of protest rallies; Archbishop Tutu's house; the memorial to children killed in the fight for freedom; the Mandela house, disputed between supporters of Nelson Mandela and his estranged ex-wife Winnie (sentenced to 5 years imprisonment in April 2003 on 25 counts of theft and 43 of fraud); the shebeens (beer halls); markets selling anything from CDs to tribal medicines; and "Millionaires' Row", grand houses built for successful black entrepreneurs when they had no choice as to where to live. On the edges of Soweto, thousands of minibuses (mainly unlicensed) gather to transport its residents to their jobs in Johannesburg.

drift to the cities, the state forced the black population to live in designated suburbs.

A notorious result of this policy is Soweto, with its endless rows of identical single-storey houses—built on one level to facilitate police intervention and the disbanding of anti-apartheid political groups. Unfortunately, the housing provided did little to decrease crime or to improve the lot of the blacks. Almost 2 million people live in this township, a few enjoying considerable wealth while most suffer grinding poverty.

Pretoria

Less than an hour by road from Johannesburg is the political capital of South Africa, Pretoria. A pleasant place to spend a few days, Pretoria is less exciting than Johannesburg, but it boasts a wider range of historical attractions and is arguably less crime-ridden. It was named after Andries Pretorius, the general who won the great victory over the Zulus at Blood River in 1838. His son became president of the Transvaal.

Pretoria is today a peaceful administrative centre and university city. It became the capital of the Boer Republic of Transvaal in 1855. Its development accelerated with the gold rush of 1886, followed by the diamond rush at Cullinan, situated only 20 km (12½ miles) away to the east.

In the Footsteps of Paul Kruger

Pretoria is linked to the history of Paul Kruger, last president of Transvaal, who was born in 1825 in the Cape Colony, participated in the Great Trek at age 10, and died in exile in Switzerland in 1904. His home in Church Street has been turned into a museum displaying furniture and objects which belonged to the legendary statesman, as well as mementoes of the Boer War.

In Church Square, to the east, a statue of Kruger by Anton van Wouw stands in the shadow of imposing buildings. In the southwest corner of the square, the Council Chamber was the seat of the old Boer Republic.

State Theatre

To the east of Church Square, the State Theatre is home to a magnificent artistic complex of six auditoria. Guided tours are available. This vast temple devoted to the arts is used not only for operatic, dramatic and choral productions, but also for ballet performances and symphony concerts. Try to visit on Saturdays when a lively flea market buzzes outside.

City Hall

Further south, the old City Hall stands out on Paul Kruger Avenue. It is a splendid piece of Victorian grandeur: the clock tower has a peal of 32 bells accompanied by an organ of 6,800 pipes. Statues of Andries Pretorius, the pioneer general, and his son Marthinus, the president, stand in front of the building.

The Museum of Natural History, opposite, is one of the best in South Africa, with displays of mammals and other species, exhibits relating to early man, and the definitive collection of stuffed South African birds.

To see living examples, visit the National Zoological Gardens, in a 600 ha (1,500-acre) park just north of the centre.

Union Buildings

In the centre of a park laid out with handsome gardens, the red sandstone Union Buildings (1913) designed by Sir Herbert Baker are the administrative seat of government and home to the National Archives. In 1994 this was the scene of the investiture of President Nelson Mandela before 42 heads of state and 5,000 other foreign dignitaries.

Voortrekker Monument

Even this event failed to totter the Voortrekker Monument, on a hilltop south of the city. This imposing granite edifice symbolizes the era of the Great Trek (1835–38) and the intransigence of the Boers in their fight for independence. The outer wall is a carved stone relief of a circle of covered ox-wagons, the famed laager of the Voortrekkers. Below the monument is a museum of pioneer life.

Cullinan

Some 50 minutes by road east of Pretoria, the fabled Cullinan diamond mine is still in operation. The vertical pipe of heavy blue diamond-bearing rock at the Premier mine is the oldest deposit of kimberlite known to exist—a trifling 1,700 million years old. One quarter of all stones worldwide of more than 400 carats uncut weight have come from this mine. This is where the Star of Africa and other gigantic gems originated.

Visits are closely supervised. Although you will not be encouraged to help yourself to a few

Symmetry and bright colours are the hallmarks of Ndebele women artists.

kimberlite souvenirs, it is possible to buy some small pieces at the mine shop—said to contain minute diamonds, sometimes.

Kwa-Ndebele

Northeast of Pretoria, near Hammanskraal, the former "homeland" of Kwa-Ndebele offers a unique opportunity to see something of the local people's traditional way of life. Visitors are welcomed to striking villages made up of huts gaily painted in bright colours.

Ndebele art is based on the straight line, even if the occasional circle does creep into the dazzling display of superimposed diagonals, squares and rectangles. Painters express their talent on the outside walls of their dwellings, while craftswomen use the designs to create jewellery, blankets and clothing, which have even inspired dress designers of Cape Town and Johannesburg.

Married women wear heavy bronze rings around their arms, necks and ankles, though these tend to be replaced nowadays by thick coils made up of thousands of tiny coloured beads. Some women also wear robes with beads woven into the fabric. House-painting is essentially a female occupation; the men have drearier work down the nearby mines. 21

This farming and mining region is best known for two adjacent but contrasting attractions: the glitzy, artificial Sun City and wilder Pilanesberg National Park. At Mafikeng (former Mafeking) there are still reminders of the Boer War, where British defenders led by Baden-Powell were besieged for 217 days.

Sun City

The somewhat surreal "Lost City", 150 km (94 miles) from Johannesburg, was designed to provide white South Africans with a local version of Las Vegas and the chance to wallow in conspicuous consumption. Just two hours by hotel courtesy bus from Johannesburg International Airport, Sun City is devoted entirely to pleasure. The promoter of this complex, Sol Kerzner, found a way round South African laws which banned gambling, by building it in the former "independent" state of Bophuthatswana. The son of Russian immigrants, born in a modest part of Johannesburg, he takes pride in the fact that the project gave jobs to some 60,000 workers and that every day 16 million litres (4,230,000 gallons) of water is recycled to supply the fountains. Tourists, artists, entertainers and "beautiful people" from all over

the world come to lose a fortune in the casinos, see the shows and, when sated with man-made entertainment, go "on safari" to commune with nature at the nearby Pilanesberg Park. Everyone can fulfil fantasies of opulence swimming or dining in a universe of lakes rippled by artificial waves, of waterslides and huge cascades; playing a round of desert golf on a course greener than an English lawn; sailing; water-skiing and playing tennis. Love it or hate it, you won't remain indifferent to Sun City's extravagance.

Pilanesberg National Park

Sun City and several other hotels fringe the Pilanesberg National Park, a tract of wooded savannah centred on Lake Mankwe that supports abundant wildlife—including reintroduced lion, elephant and rhino—and guarantees an unforgettable photo safari. Located on the verge of the Kalahari biome, Pilanesberg supports numerous western bird species at the eastern extent of their range, notably the stunning (and vocal) crimson-breasted shrike—a good selection can be seen in the walk-in aviary at the main entrance gate. Birds and mammals are most active in the early morning, so it's worth staying in a chalet or tent within the park, which is dotted with strange rock formations of volcanic origin. Guided night drives offer a good chance of encountering nocturnal shy creatures such as brown hyena, aardwolf and genet.

The wooden wheels of the Boer ox-carts first opened the great highway which today runs from Pretoria to the river on the Zimbabwe border for which Limpopo (formerly Northern) Province is named. The region is steeped in history: ruins and remains emerge from dense forest intersected by waterfalls and torrents rich in trout. Tea plantations and vast orchards complement the subtropical vegetation.

Polokwane

The first town you meet on the long N1 highway from Pretoria is Bela-Bela (formerly Warmbaths), known for its hot springs. But there are still another hundred or so kilometres to go before you reach Polokwane (formerly Pietersburg), an agricultural centre and the biggest town of the region, founded in 1886. In the open-air museum at Bakone Malapa, 9 km (6 miles) outside of town, you can visit a kraal, or traditional village, and learn something of the way of life of the northern Sothos.

Louis Trichardt

If you follow the N1 north towards Zimbabwe, you will reach Louis Trichardt, a historic town that takes its name from one of the most famous Voortrekkers. South of the town, the Ben Lavin Nature Reserve is home to numerous species of animals and birds. To the northwest, the Soutpansberg trail crosses a forested range of mountains covered with rare trees, palm-like cycads, tree ferns, podocarpus conifers and wild figs.

Musina and Mapungubwe Hill

North of Louis Trichardt, the N1 passes by several striking baobab trees, all of which are national monuments. A superb specimen can be spotted from the road, 5 km (3 miles) before the small town of Musina (formerly Messina).

Overlooking the Limpopo River, some 75 km (46 miles) northwest of Musina, is Mapungubwe Hill, topped by the extensive remains of an indigenous stone city that flourished from AD 950, and which have recently been opened to tourists. Several artefacts unearthed at the site—most famously two gold statues of rhinoceros—indicate that this ancient city's wealth was built on gold, which was mined locally, transported by land to Indian Ocean ports such as Sofala and Kilwa, then shipped to Arabia. The stone city, whose contemporary name goes unrecorded, was abandoned circa AD 1200, when its residents evidently relocated further north to build Great Zimbabwe.

Tzaneen

The main roads to the northern section of the Kruger National Park lead from Polokwane through the Tzaneen region. The most beautiful route involves a detour over the Magoebaskloof Pass, crossing forests and tea plantations on the way. It takes in the pretty village of Haernertsburg, smothered in springtime by azaleas and flowering cherry trees.

Other sights on the way to Tzaneen are the artificial lake of the Ebenezer Dam surrounded by pine forest and eucalyptus plantations, and waterfalls at Debengeni, 80 m (262 ft) high.

Tzaneen is a charming place for an overnight stop in the middle of tobacco and coffee plantations, orchards, nut groves and vegetable farms.

◤ MPUMALANGA
Blyde River Canyon, Pilgrim's Rest, Nelspruit,
Kruger National Park, Sabi Sands Game Reserve

The countryside of Mpumalanga, formerly Eastern Transvaal, is well worth a visit in its own right; it lies conveniently on the main route from Pretoria or Johannesburg to the Kruger Park's southern section.

Blyde River Canyon

The Blyde River Nature Reserve is a botanical paradise, with rare plant species such as aloes, cycads, orchids and ferns to be seen as well as an abundance of wildlife including several vociferous monkey species. The Blyde River Canyon, with sheer cliffs of red and yellow sandstone rising to 800 m (2,600 ft) in places, cuts through the reserve for 26 km (16 miles). A number of walking trails offer tours of any length up to several days, with overnight huts provided. Signs of human occupation dating from the Stone Age have been found in the Echo Caves, on private property a 20-minute drive west of the reserve.

Huts and Potholes

The most stunning viewpoint over the Blyde River, situated alongside a trunk road, is the Three Rondavels, where three enormous rocks in the shape of African huts rise up from the cliffs some 700 m (2,300 ft) on the opposite side of the canyon. At the confluence of this waterway with the Treur River, Bourke's Luck Potholes, scoured out by the staggering force of the water during the summer rains, impress with their perfect circular shape. And from God's Window, you can look between the rocks as if from a casement in the sky to view the savannah of the lowveld, which sweeps eastward towards the Kruger National Park. Not far away, the granite column of Pinnacle Rock rises like an exclamation mark above the delights of this favourite region of walkers and horsemen.

A Water World

The waters themselves play no small part in nature's spectacle. The magnificent 80-m (263-ft) Berlin Falls plunging from the mountain into a deep pool and the nearby horseshoe Lisbon Falls both afford extensive views over the wild, rocky landscapes of the canyon.

The most-visited falls of the area are the twin cascades which pour into the Mac Mac Pools. The curious name is said to come from the large number of Scots who came to seek their fortune during the gold rush. The pure

An observation platform has been built to view the Berlin Falls in all their splendour.

waters of these forest pools offer a blissful swim after a hot drive. Unlike most rivers in the region, they are free from the bilharzia parasite.

Pilgrim's Rest

The small town of Pilgrim's Rest was built in 1873 by the first gold rush pioneers. For practical purposes the gold finally ran out a century later, but what might easily have become a ghost town was carefully preserved. The historic atmosphere is maintained in an old mine, restored 19th-century tin houses and rudimentary shops. Some of the miners' cottages have been converted into hotel rooms, while demonstrations of gold-panning help to recreate the good old days.

To the east, Sabie is a pretty forestry town situated at the base of the region's tallest peak, Mount Anderson.

Nelspruit

Nelspruit is the modern capital of Mpumalanga, a centre of production for nuts, subtropical fruit and citrus varieties, lying between the Kruger National Park and Swaziland. The Lowveld Botanical Garden, set on the banks of the Crocodile River on the northern outskirts of Nelspruit, is planted with an interesting selection of 27 tropical trees—including baobabs and cycads—and is also host to a wide variety of colourful birds.

The road west back to Pretoria passes through the territory of the Southern Ndebele peoples. At the Botshabelo Nature Reserve, 15 km (9 miles) from Middelburg, a village and museum are dedicated to the Ndebele's appealing crafts, while a small game sanctuary protects, among other things, a herd of the endemic black wildebeest.

Kruger National Park

The Kruger National Park is South Africa's premier game viewing destination, home to 138 mammal species including aardvark, buffalo, cheetah, elephant, giraffe, hippopotamus, hyena, impala, leopard, lion, rhinoceros—and so on through the alphabet all the way to zebra. More than 100 different types of reptile are present, too. Extending over 19,000 sq km (7,335 sq miles), the park has recently become the cornerstone of a much larger trans-frontier park extending into Mozambique and Zimbabwe.

Divided between the provinces of Limpopo and Mpumalanga, the park contains around a dozen large rest camps, most of which offer comfortable and affordable bungalows with all modern conveniences, as well as campsites, shops and restaurants. Unlike many other African parks, the Kruger is also very easy to get around in a rented or private vehicle, with in excess of 2,500 km (1,560 miles) of well-maintained asphalt and dirt roads to explore.

Southern Region

The park is conventionally divided into three zones, each with a distinct ecology and character. The southern section is the most popular with locals and tourists, not least because of its relative proximity to Gauteng and wide choice of accommodation. Rest camps include Skakuza (the largest and best-equipped in the park), Lower Sabie (unmatched location for game drives), Crocodile Bridge (small, intimate, and in an area known for rhino sightings), Pretoriuskop and Bergendal. Characterized by dense acacia scrub and transected by the Sabi River, the southern sector probably offers the best general game viewing in the park, with lion, wild dog, elephant and rhinoceros often seen alongside large herds of greater kudu and impala.

Central Region

More open in character, the central region is still reasonably accessible from Gauteng, and has some of the nicest rest camps in the park. Satara, though rather large and impersonal, lies in excellent lion and cheetah country, often

frequented by large herds of zebra and wildebeest. Olifants, perched on a cliff above the synonymous and aptly named river, is arguably the most spectacular camp of the lot. On the banks of the Letaba River, the camp of the same name is the favourite of many regulars, for its intimate feel, lovely setting and abundant game.

Northern Region

Favoured by the cognoscenti is the somewhat remote northern sector, which is characterized by thick mopane woodland, and serviced by only a few small rest camps, of which Shingwedzi and Punda Maria both stand out. Although the northern circuit harbours lesser densities of game, its wilderness character more than compensates, and the concentrations of animals and birds along the Pafuri and Shingwedzi Rivers can be astounding.

Birdlife

The Kruger is mainly visited for its large mammals, but it's also a prime birding spot, with over 500 species recorded, of which the lovely lilac-breasted roller and white-fronted bee-eater routinely delight visitors. The park is a stronghold for several large birds —martial eagle, ground hornbill, secretary bird and kori bustard, for instance—that are increasingly rare outside protected areas.

Sabi Sands Game Reserve

Sabi Sands is a jointly administered block of private reserves that shares its unfenced eastern border with the southern Kruger Park, and protects a broadly similar range of large mammals and birds. Several small luxury lodges lie within the reserve—the world-renowned Mala Mala, Sabi Sabi and Londolozi among them—offering the alluring combination of five-star bush accommodation, superb food and wine, and probably the best "Big Five" game-viewing in Africa.

Most of the lodges offer a similar package: two daily game drives in an open safari vehicle, accompanied by a knowledgeable ranger and experienced tracker, following the rough roads that characterize the reserve, occasionally crashing through the bush in pursuit of a special sighting. The reserve is famed for its superb big cat sightings: it's not unusual to see lion, cheetah and leopard in the course of one game drive, and the latter are incredibly habituated. Rhino, wild dog and elephant are also regularly encountered. The more intrepid can go on a bush walk with an expert guide, not only a good opportunity to concentrate on plants, birds and insects, but also offering a chance of a heart-stopping close encounter with a lion or buffalo.

KwaZulu-Natal assumed its present shape in 1994 following the amalgamation of the apartheid-era province of Natal and the nominally self-governing former "homeland" of KwaZulu (literally Place of the Zulu). The western boundary of KwaZulu-Natal is formed by the majestic Drakensberg Mountains, while the east coast is washed by the waters of the Indian Ocean. Although Vasco da Gama sailed past present-day Durban on Christmas Day of 1497—and named the port Natalia—only in the 1820s did the first European traders, hunters and ivory merchants settle in the area. Port Natal and its nascent harbour town were subsequently renamed Durban in honour of Sir Benjamin d'Urban, the governor of the Cape responsible for the British annexation of the area, but Da Gama's original name has been retained for the province. Many of the early engagements of the Anglo-Boer War were fought in the western part of Natal: Colenso, Spioenkop and the siege of Ladysmith.

Durban

Occupied by the Boers during the Great Trek, then retaken by the British, Durban is the nation's largest port. Impregnated with the scent of spices, this is the biggest city in KwaZulu-Natal and the third biggest in South Africa with more than a million inhabitants. Durban is also a sort of Indian Ocean version of Miami. You might easily get the impression that the entire population is devoted to sun-and-sea worship. Surfers brave the breakers all along its endless string of dazzling beaches, while golfers confront the perfectly tended fairways.

The Sea Front

Durban's sea front is vaguely reminiscent of the Bay of Nice, or Copacabana. Its Golden Mile stretches for not just one but five miles (8 km), a parade of international restaurants, hotels and well-guarded beaches. An amusement park with miniature trains, boat-trips and merry-go-rounds enlivens this world of concrete high-rises and swimming pools, made colourful by the stalls of Zulu women selling handicrafts. Rickshaw drivers in Zulu dress ply up and down the beach front.

The formerly run-down port area is undergoing attractive redevelopment. Harbour cruises are a highlight. 31

Sea World and Reptiles

Families visiting this urban solarium will enjoy calling in at Sea World, where a team of dolphins, killer whales, seals and penguins go through their paces. A bewildering variety of marine life is on display, including tropical fish, sharks and turtles.

Further north, Snake Park at North Beach houses 100 species of snake, including 60 from Africa, plus crocodiles and iguanas.

The Indian Connection

As the most easterly of South Africa's large cities, Durban is fittingly the place to find Indian markets. Victoria Street Market, set up in a domed building that looks like a Maharajah's Palace, is an absolute must. Its stalls and shops offer all the spices of the Orient—and quite a few of its manufactured goods, too.

The oriental influence is further illustrated by sanctuaries such as the vast golden-domed Jumah mosque on Grey Street, and the Indian Temple of Understanding further south at Chatsworth, near the road to the airport. Built by the Krishna Consciousness Movement, the temple is a genuine masterpiece of religious architecture, with an opulent interior. The Indian population first came to South Africa in the 1860s to work in the sugar-cane plantations. The population now numbers over a million and is influential in local commerce. Mahatma Gandhi began his political career here as a lawyer campaigning for the rights of Indian people.

A Stroll through Town

The impressive City Hall marks the centre of Durban and houses the Public Library, the Durban Museum of Art and the Museum of Natural History, which has a good collection of ornithological exhibits, including one stuffed dodo. The nearby Natal Theatre complex is the centre of the province's dramatic art. The business area behind the seafront is livelier by night than by day, with its many bars and clubs. A stroll through the town can be rounded off by boarding a boat at Victoria Embankment for a trip round the harbour. From the water you can take a look at the Da Gama Clock, a gift to the city of Durban from the people of Portugal in 1897 to commemorate the 400th anniversary of Vasco da Gama's arrival on these shores.

Zululand

Northern KwaZulu-Natal, generally referred to as Zululand, is one of the most exciting parts of South Africa to explore in a private vehi-

A Durban speciality: a Zulu taxi rank.

cle, boasting fine game reserves, as well as a succession of lush subtropical beaches—and, of course, lying at the historical heart of the great Zulu Kingdom. Whereas the peaceful Ndebele are appreciated for the artistic skills of the women, their Zulu cousins, despite many social and linguistic similarities, are chiefly known for their warlike qualities. There is little doubt that Zulu warriors are among the most fearsome, the most colourful and the most impressive in all of southern Africa.

Hluhluwe-Umfolozi Game Reserve

The largest and oldest of the Zululand game reserves, Hluhluwe and Umfolozi (both named after the rivers that run through them) were proclaimed separately in 1897, but are now linked by a corridor of state-owned land and managed as a single 100,000-hectare unit.

The Hluhluwe-Umfolozi complex is best known for its critical role in rhino conservation. White rhino would today almost certainly be extinct were it not for Umfolozi—when the reserve was proclaimed, only 30 survived in the wild in South Africa—while Hluhluwe has long been a major stronghold for black rhino. Not only does this reserve protect the world's highest densities of wild rhinoceros, but almost 5,000 of its rhino (including the founders of the present-day Kruger Park population) have been relocated to other game reserves over the years.

Hluhluwe in particular is one of the most scenic of South African reserves, an undulating land-

---

ZULU DANCING

Zulu games and dances are intertwined, children being introduced very early in life to their traditional tribal choreography. Every gesture is imbued with significance and translates an idea. Dances are the means of making a covenant with the gods, of consecrating the initiation of boys and of girls into adulthood, of recounting an adventure, of celebrating an exploit. The rhythms bring happiness and symbolize hope.

While dancing, the Zulu child plays at being a soldier, bringing to life again the rites of the glorious warriors of old. Small boys, each holding his shield and a stick, sometimes even an assegai, take their weight on one leg and swing the other high to the sky before crashing it back down to the ground, as if trying to crack the very earth wide open.

scape of rolling hills covered in dense acacia scrub, running down to the jungle-fringed banks of the Hluhluwe River. You'd be unfortunate to spend a day in either reserve without bumping into rhino—white are more common and less secretive than black—as well as elephant, buffalo, zebra and nyala antelope. Lion, leopard and wild dog are present, too, though sightings are less reliable than in the Kruger/Sabi Sands complex. Birdlife is fabulous, and two short self-guided walks, leading from the main rest camps, supplement the excellent guided walks that head deeper into rhino country.

Phinda Resource Reserve

Zululand's answer to the private reserves of Sabi Sands, Phinda was founded in 1991 when Conservation Corporation Africa (the same company that owns the legendary Londolozi) acquired some 14,000 hectares of degraded farmland and hunting concessions abutting the Greater St Lucia Wetland. Over the next couple of years, elephant, lion, rhino, cheetah and buffalo were re-introduced to the fenced reserve, which already protected small populations of leopard and various antelope, and four small, exclusive lodges were constructed. One of the most carefully managed reserves in Africa, Phinda is too compact and con-

tained to be regarded as true wilderness, but the expertly guided game drives—in open vehicles—are reliably superlative. The odds of seeing the Big Five over a couple of days are very good, and close encounters with cheetah are something of a speciality.

Ndumo Game Reserve

Nudged against the Mozambique border, this small reserve is primarily known for its diverse avifauna. Regarded by many as the country's finest birdwatching site, Ndumo's dense scrub and fig forests harbour numerous species with a limited range in South Africa, and the network of rivers, swamps and lakes teem with water associated birds. Boat trips from the park's only lodge reliably offer dentist-eye views of hippos and crocs, while game drives and guided walks often result in close-up encounters with giraffe, black rhino and nyala antelope.

Tembe Elephant Reserve

Situated a short distance east of Ndumo, Tembe was proclaimed and fenced off in 1983 to protect a herd of about 80 elephant that formerly ranged between South Africa and Mozambique. Serviced by a small tented camp, this reserve harbours several other large mammals, as well as many bird species more normally associated with Ndumo—there's some talk of linking the two reserves eventually. Access is by 4-wheel drive vehicle only.

Mkuzi Game Reserve

Another compact but thrilling game reserve, Mkuzi is a reliable place to see rhino, giraffe and the lovely nyala antelope. A series of hides overlooking the waterholes is particularly rewarding for photography in the early dry season, when the water attracts a steady stream of game. A beautiful lake in the south of the reserve, encircled by tall stands of yellow fever trees and low hills, is scenically reminiscent of East Africa's Rift Valley, and often harbours large numbers of hippo and pelican. The nearby fig forest is a treat for birders, as is the self-guided walk around the main rest camp.

Northern Zululand Coast

Situated off the coast of northern KwaZulu-Natal, Africa's most southerly coral reefs support a wide range of colourful tropical fish, and Sodwana Bay in particular is very popular with South African anglers, divers and snorkellers. The expansive, pristine sandy beaches that characterize this stretch of Indian Ocean coastline also form an important breeding side for endangered marine turtles, while the coastal scrub hosts several localized birds and

troops of monkey. Lake Sibaya, a short distance inland, is—incredibly—the largest natural freshwater body in South Africa, with 200 ot more hippo resident. Tourist development in the area, not resort-like in any conventional sense, is epitomized by the game lodge-like feel of the superb, exclusive Rocktail Bay Lodge, close to the Mozambique border.

Greater Saint Lucia Wetland Park

Proclaimed a UNESCO World Heritage Site in 1999, St Lucia is South Africa's largest estuarine system, dominated by a lagoon 50 km (30 miles) long that is fed by half a dozen rivers and divided from the Indian Ocean by a terrestrial sliver of tall dunes swathed in lush coastal forest. The village of St Lucia, with a fabulous location at the estuary mouth, is the obvious base for exploring the area. In addition to having a fine beach, albeit more popular with anglers than sunbathers, the village is equipped with plenty of accommodation. It also forms the starting point for launch trips on the estuary (prodigious hippos, crocs and waterbirds) and for self-guided walks among the zebra and wildebeest that frequent a small bordering game reserve.

A superbly scenic drive on an indifferent road between the estuary and the ocean leads north from Saint Lucia village to the idyllic beach and rest camp at Cape Vidal, passing en route through grassy swamps frequented by large herds of reedbuck and a series of bird hides overlooking estuary. On the western shore of the estuary, Charters Creek rest camp stands in a patch of thick coastal scrub inhabited by warthog, the diminutive red duiker and a variety of forest birds—listen out for the cat-in-a-mangle wailing of the preposterous trumpeter hornbill. For keen walkers, the nearby False Bay Reserve is transected by two excellent day trails through a tract of dunes and coastal bush teeming with large mammals and birds.

Ulundi

The former administrative capital of the defunct KwaZulu "homeland", Ulundi lies inland of the Hluhluwe-Umfolozi Game Reserve about 200 km (125 miles) northeast of Durban. Of greater interest than the inherently unremarkable former capital is KwaZulu Cultural and Historical Museum, built on the site of King Cetshwayo's royal enclosure at Ondoni, a mere 5 km (3 miles) from Ulundi. Razed by British troops in 1879, Cetshwayo's enclosure is now partially restored, while the main museum building houses an absorbing miscellany

of Zulu artefacts and historical displays—and inexpensive on-site accommodation in traditional Zulu beehive huts!

Shakaland and other cultural villages

Several traditional Zulu villages (*kraal* in Afrikaans) may be visited in KwaZulu/Natal Province. The most established of these is Shakaland, 15 km (9 miles) from Eshowe and about 150 km (94 miles) north of Durban. King Shaka (1788–1828) has been called "Africa's Napoleon". His kraal was completely recreated for the film *Shaka Zulu* and is now run by a hotel chain—you can book accommodation. The traditions and costumes of the Zulu people are presented in a happy atmosphere. You can sample local food and watch the many demonstrations of Zulu dances and rites. Despite historical inaccuracies, the village is attractive and provides employment for many local people.

Shakaland can become very overcrowded with day trippers in the high season, but two other conceptually similar hotels in the Eshowe region offer an equally insightful and somewhat lower key cultural experience. Kwabekitunga is a small, private lodge where visitors can spend time with a traditional Zulu family that's lived in the area for as long as anybody can remember. More memorable still is Simunye, spectacularly set on a cliff overlooking a traditional Zulu kraal—visitors are transferred to the lodge in a traditional ox-wagon, and the more adventurous can opt to sleep in a hut within the kraal rather than in the more conventional tourist rooms!

Military history buffs will want to visit the Zulu War battlefields, including Isandhlwana and Rorke's Drift. Close together, east of Dundee, they were the scenes of many acts of courage as well as disastrous losses on both sides. You will find local guided tours and maps at the tourist offices.

From Eshowe to Durban

In the small neighbouring town of Eshowe, the first administrative centre of British Zululand, the British fort of Nongqai, built in 1883, has been refurbished as the Historical Museum of Zululand. The lush, shady Dhlinza Forest Reserve, situated in the heart of this pretty town, is a good place to see the tiny blue duiker and a wide selection of forest birds.

Further south, the Umlalazi Nature Reserve, bordering the small resort town of Mtunzini, might be rather low-key by comparison to the game reserves of northern Zululand, but it still has much to offer keen walkers. Particularly rewarding is a foot trail through the mangroves, where one is likely to encounter hermit crabs, mudskippers (a fish that can live on land) and the localized mangrove kingfisher—most likely to be detected by its shrill call. A stand of raffia palms within the reserve is the only breeding site in the country for the majestic palmnut vulture.

Although most tours return to Durban along the N2 highway in a matter hours, it is also possible to take the road through the interior, allowing two days for the complete circuit including the visit to Shakaland. Driving through the hilly country of Zululand you will see other communities and more kraals such as Assagai Safari Park and PheZulu by taking the route through the Valley of a Thousand Hills between Pietermaritzburg and the coast.

South Coast

Between Durban and Port Edward you have at least a hundred resorts to choose from. Well worth considering are Amanzimtoti and the Nyoni Rocks with 7 km (4 miles) of safe beaches; Margate, which gets the vote of the young crowd for its lively nightlife; and Shelly Beach for its abundance of shells.

If you need a break from the sea, the Vernon Crookes Nature Reserve is a haven for many birds, 39

together with eland, blue wildebeest, impala and zebra. The Oribi Gorge, 24 km (15 miles) long, shelters antelope, leopard and baboons between its majestic sandstone cliffs studded with euphorbia; eagles soar above.

Wild Coast

You can continue south beyond Port Edward along the spectacular Wild Coast as far as East London, crossing the old frontier of the former Transkei "homeland" on the way. Along some stretches the violence of the confrontation of ocean and mountain is simply breathtaking. The pounding of wave against rock has created a giant hollow in the cliff face at Hole in the Wall near Mncwasa Point and Coffee Bay. The most beautiful parts of this coast have been made into nature reserves, but access is not always easy as the topography has prevented construction of a road that clings to the shore.

Pietermaritzburg

Smaller and far sleepier than Durban, Pietermaritzburg is nevertheless the provincial capital of KwaZulu-Natal. Nestled in a lush, misty valley in the southern part

The coast near Coffee Bay has been battered and hammered by the forces of nature.

of the province, the compact town centre has retained many of its old buildings, giving something of the atmosphere of the era of the Voortrekkers who arrived at this fertile site in 1837. The settlement they founded, with wide streets and pretty gardens, was named in honour of two of their leaders, Piet Retief and Gerrit Maritz.

Around Town

The Voortrekker House, the oldest two-storey dwelling in town, has been carefully restored and authentically furnished.

In 1842 the British annexed the young Natal Republic, installed a military garrison and chose Pietermaritzburg as the administrative centre of the new colony of Natal. A good number of buildings dating from the colonial era survive, including mosques and Hindu temples of the Indian traders and the Macrorie House Museum containing furniture and clothing from the Victorian age.

The town hall, a Victorian building where 12 bells ring out from the top of its 47-m (155-ft) tower, is said to be the largest all-brick building in the southern hemisphere. Edwardian and Victorian façades rise above narrow lanes paved in the same red brick, and even the schools have made it a point of honour to maintain the great British traditions.

A broad panorama of the town can be seen from the belvedere and landmark table at World's View on the Howick road, at an altitude of 305 m (1,000 ft).

Walks and Drives

The lush countryside surrounding Pietermaritzburg caters to every interest. The Green Belt Trail can be followed on foot or on horseback through areas of abundant plant and animal life. The Midlands Meander is a circuit through the Midlands towns and villages where there are many delightful restaurants, art galleries, and craft centres featuring weaving and pottery-making, notably around the town of Nottingham Road.

More than 200 species of bird have been recorded in the Umgeni Valley, while the magnificent Howick Falls, overlooked by the small town of the same name, plunge from a height of 100 m (328 ft) in an unspoilt setting with plentiful wildlife.

The Drakensberg

All along the Lesotho frontier, in a land of highland horsemen, the rugged outline of the Drakensberg (Dragon's Mountain) includes some of the highest peaks of South Africa. Twelve of them rise to more than 3,000 m (9,800 ft). In the foothills of these vertiginous walls of basalt, superb nature reserves provide accommodation 41 in all categories for walkers and climbers. The Royal Natal National Park alone is worth the journey to the Drakensberg.

Royal Natal National Park

The park's natural amphitheatre, a basalt arc 8 km (5 miles) long, is guarded by towering peaks, the Sentinel, 3,165 m (10,400 ft) and the Eastern Buttress, 3,047 m (9,997 ft). Spring Mountain, 3,284 m (10,770 ft), is the source of the River Tugela which falls more than 2,000 m (6,560 ft) in a series of cascades down to the plateau below.

While you walk the park trails it is not unusual to encounter Zulu women cutting reeds for basket-weaving. You don't have to be a mountain-climber to enjoy the park; there are easy walking trails, as well as more challenging routes.

Giant's Castle

In the middle of the Drakensberg, the Giant's Castle Game Reserve supports a range of antelope—notably eland. A major attraction for ornithologists is a so-called "vulture restaurant" where carrion is left out to attract to scavenging birds. The endemic Cape vulture and rare bearded vulture (or lammergeier) are both regular visitors to the site.

However, the reserve is chiefly known for its many caves decorated with Bushman (San) rock paintings.

Richly supplied with game and with plentiful water, the Drakensberg Mountains were once a safe haven for the peaceful San who inhabited southern Africa for thousands of years before the arrival of the first Europeans. Chased from their hunting grounds, initially by more warlike pastoral tribes and later by European settlers, these hardy hunter-gatherers left behind a rich collection of rock art illustrating the essentials of their daily life. In rust-red, purple-brown and ochre, their murals most frequently depict men and animals (usually eland), warriors engaged in battle, or shaman performing mystical trance rituals. Experts say the most ancient of these works of art were created 27,000 years ago; more recent paintings depicting ox-wagons and the like demonstrate that the artists were still active at the time of the Great Trek.

One of the most fascinating panels contains 546 paintings and is only 2 km (a little over a mile) from a camp where you can stay overnight in a thatched hut. In another cave, as many as 750 rock paintings have been counted.

The verdant landscape of the Drakensberg.

The Free State, founded more than a century ago, was originally named the Orange Free State after the Orange River on its southern boundary. It is a vast region, occupying the highveld of the central plateau to the south of Johannesburg, and sharing its frontier with Gauteng, Mpumalanga, KwaZulu/Natal, Eastern and Northern Cape and North-West provinces, as well as the independent Lesotho enclave. The granary of the nation, the Free State is characterized by immense plains of wheat and maize, and it is also rich in natural resources such as gold, diamonds, uranium and—more humbly—coal.

Bloemfontein

The prosperous city of Bloemfontein, capital of this attractive province, was founded by *trekboeren* in the 1840s as capital of the Orange Free State. It served as a centre of British operations during the Anglo-Boer War. The name literally means "spring of flowers", though it could well have been named after one Jan Bloem, who lived here before the Voortrekkers. The column and mosaic of the Fontein (fountain) mark the spring which was the origin of the town.

Now a museum, the First Raadsaal, a thatched adobe construction with beaten dung floor, dates from 1849 and is the oldest of a handful of 19th-century buildings close to the central square. The Legislative Assembly (Volksraad) used to meet here, but it became too small for the flourishing community and three more raadsaals were built in succession. The Third Raadsaal houses the National Afrikaans Literary museum.

Bloemfontein is the judicial capital of South Africa. The Appeal Court, seat of the country's highest judicial authority, boasts several richly furnished rooms. The old Presidency, which was built in 1885 in the Victorian style now houses a collection of presidential documents tracing the history of the Boer Republic of Orange Free State.

Before the British occupation of the town in 1900, the Assembly met in the Fourth Raadsaal, a handsome red-brick building with Doric columns and a domed tower and still in use as a government building.

A 36.5-m (120-ft) obelisk, the National Women's Memorial honours the 26,000 women and children who died of disease in the concentration camps of the Anglo-Boer War (1899–1902).

Willem Pretorius Game Reserve

To the north, close to the Johannesburg road, the Willem Pretorius Game Reserve, encircling the great lake formed by the Allemanskraal Dam, is particularly rich in white rhinoceros. They happily coexist with many other wildlife species. Because of the sparse vegetation it's relatively easy to see and photograph the animals, and a high hill dominating the savannah makes a perfect observation point.

Superficially similar, white and black rhinoceros can readily be distinguished from each other by the respective shapes of their mouths. The white rhino has wide, square lips suited to cropping grass, while the slightly smaller (and significantly more pugnacious) black rhino has a narrow mouth, overhung by a hooked upper lip, reflecting its browsing habits.

Ladybrand

The Catharina Brand Museum at Ladybrand displays a collection of fossils, painted rocks, Bushman tools and musical instruments which date from the Stone Age. They may inspire you to visit some of the archaeological sites of the region, among which

Rose Cottage Cave and Modderpoort Cave Church are the most significant. Countless scenic beauty spots stretch along the nearby frontier with Lesotho as far as Harrismith.

Golden Gate National Park

The Sterkfontein Dam Reserve draws ornithologists and anglers, but the best place for bird-watching is Golden Gate, named after a spectacular rock formation, and situated at an altitude of above 2,000 m (6,600 ft) on the northwest slopes of the Drakensberg. In a prodigious mountain setting, Cape vultures, black eagles, bearded vultures (or lammergeiers) and numerous other species produce a thrilling fly-past.

Clarens

Haunt of artists, the small and picturesque town of Clarens offers a fine view of the Maluti Mountains. The town's most unusual sight is the so-called Cinderella Castle, an incongruous blue-turreted affair made out of 55,000 beer bottles.

Brandwater Hiking Trail

Fouriesburg marks the start of the Brandwater Hiking Trail, a path which leads to the Salpeterkrans limestone cave, the largest in the southern hemisphere. The entire region caters chiefly to hikers.

Landlocked—in fact, surrounded on all sides by South African soil—Lesotho is a small, mountainous and predominantly rural country, most of which stands at an elevation of above 2,000 m. The population, estimated at 2.5 million, is comprised almost entirely of the Basotho, whose ancestors probably migrated to the highlands in the 16th century, and were consolidated into a unified nation under King Moshoeshoe in the 1820s, largely in response to the threat posed by their militant Zulu neighbours.

Never colonized as such—possibly because the land was too poor to appeal to settlers—Lesotho became a British protectorate in the late 19th century. Since independence in 1966, Lesotho has been economically dependent on its larger, wealthier neighbour, surviving on subsistence agriculture, international aid, and money sent home by migrant workers, many of them in South Africa's gold mines. Lesotho, like Swaziland, remains one of Africa's few tribally homogenous kingdoms, although it differs from Swaziland in that an elected government exists to reign in the power of the monarchy.

Inspirational montane scenery and limited development outside of major towns, together with the legendary friendliness of the blanket-clad rural Basotho, combine to make Lesotho a highly rewarding hiking and trekking destination, particularly for those seeking unforced contact with traditional cultures. For all that, few overseas tourists cross into the kingdom, if only for the simple reason that it is rather inaccessible from any established South African tourist circuit (the only surfaced roads into Lesotho approach the western border from the seldom-visited eastern Free State). Furthermore, outside the capital, few hotels meet accepted international standards. Lesotho, in essence, is a destination less suited to conventional tourism than it is to relatively intrepid independent travellers, hikers and other outdoor enthusiasts.

Maseru and surrounds

Set at an elevation of 1,650 m (4,513 ft), only 20 km (12 mikes) by road from Ladybrand in the Free State, Maseru made headlines in 1998 when South African troops controversially crossed the border to put down a revolt sparked by a contested election that had taken place earlier that year. Maseru was never the most prepossessing of capital cities, and the still visible scars of the destructive looting that followed the South African invasion have scarcely improved matters. Most travellers pass through the city as quickly as possible, but it does boast a decent tourist information office, as well as a scattering of international quality hotels should you want to stay overnight.

A more appealing place to stay is the elevated plateau of Thaba Bosiu (Mountain of Night), which is situated only 15 km (9 miles) from the modern capital. A national monument, held sacred by Basotho traditionalists, this mountain was the military stronghold from where King Moshoeshoe forged the Basotho Kingdom in the 19th century, and where he was buried after his death in 1870.

Pony treks
The most attractive way to explore the steep contours of rural Lesotho is to travel as the locals do: wrapped in a blanket on the back of a sturdy Basotho pony. One convenient base for treks is the Basotho Pony Trekking Centre, situated alongside the road to Roma, a university town 35 km (22 miles) east of Maseru. Also very popular is Malealea Lodge, which lies in a part of the southern highlands studded with mysterious rock art sites, tumbling waterfalls and rare plants such as the endemic spiral aloe. Both organizations arrange a variety of half-day treks to close-by waterfalls, as well as longer trips (up to a week in duration) generally terminating at Semonkong—site of the spectacular 190-m (623-ft) Lebihan Falls, the tallest waterfall in South Africa.

Sehlabathebe National Park
Lesotho's only national park, Sehlabathebe runs along the eastern border with the KwaZulu-Natal Drakensberg, a wild, remote landscape of timeworn sandstone formations and caves, towered over by a trio of jagged peaks known as the Three Bushmen. The main attractions of this remote park are the scenery (sweeping views to the escarpment base) and the wonderful off-the-beaten-track hiking possibilities. Some large mammals remain, too, most notably eland and grey rhebok, even the stray leopard. Birdlife includes the exquisite malachite sunbird, the mighty lammergeier and the localized bald ibis.

Halfway between Durban and the Cape of Good Hope, the Eastern Cape, both maritime and mountainous, provides a transition between the tropical exuberance of Kwa-Zulu/Natal and the delights of the Western Cape.

East London

Despite its name, the relic of its origin as a British military supply post set up in 1848, East London has a strong link to the region's German settlers who arrived ten years later. They have their own memorial monument here and, in homage to their home country, founded the nearby towns of Potsdam, Berlin and Braunschweig.

The bustling activity on East London's Buffalo River contrasts with the tranquillity of the lagoons and the long beaches of the biggest river port in South Africa.

Around Town

From East London's beginnings, some 19th- and early 20th-century buildings remain in the city centre around the junction of the main shopping thoroughfares of Oxford Street and Fleet Street. On the latter is the Old Lock Street Gaol, built in 1880 as a garrison fort and transformed into South Africa's first women's prison. Now it is a shopping centre with bars in some of the old cells.

At the north end of Oxford Street, the East London Museum features a famous coelacanth fish caught by a local fisherman in 1938. Thought to have survived 250 million years until it died out 40 million years ago, this fish, previously known to science only in fossil form, is on show here nicely stuffed, 1.6 m (5 ft) long, with all its teeth. The extinct dodo bird is also exhibited with the world's only known extant egg and a life-size model of the creature done to death by environmentally insensitive Dutch sailors. The museum also has interesting sections devoted to Xhosa tribal life and the early British and German settlers.

Over the two-tiered bridge across the mouth of the Buffalo River, Latimers Landing has been redeveloped as a shopping and restaurant area with facilities for boat and yacht cruises around the harbour.

Along the seafront esplanade overlooking Shipwreck Bay, the Aquarium boasts over 100 species of tropical fish and other marine creatures. Seals and penguins perform daily. Behind the aquarium is the German Settlers' Memorial, paying tribute to the 2,315 men, women and children who arrived here in 1857 as part of the Deutsche Legion to develop the trade potential of the port and hinterland.

Grahamstown

Best known as the site of Rhodes University and the country's premier arts festival (held over two weeks every July), Grahamstown was founded by the 1820 Settlers and it boasts several churches and other buildings dating to the mid-19th century. The 1820 Settlers Museum contains several displays and photographs relating to this period, while the Albany Museum is strong on pre-colonial history and rock art.

Port Alfred

Another 1820 Settler town that is bypassed by most international tourists, Port Alfred has a lovely beachfront location straddling the shady banks of the Kowie River estuary south of Grahamstown. An excellent overnight canoe trail follows the Kowie River through lush riverine vegetation in the Waters Meeting Nature Reserve, while the Alexandria Hiking Trail at close-by Kenton-on-Sea is of interest for its tall dunes, coastal forest, and rich birdlife.

Port Elizabeth

The beaches and resorts of Algoa Bay are justifiably the pride and joy of the industrial city of Port Elizabeth. Some Victorian buildings, notably those in Donkin Street, contrast with an otherwise unattractive industrial centre. Sir Rufane Donkin, the founder of the town, named it Port Elizabeth after his wife. Its development began in about 1820, with the arrival of 4,000 British settlers. From the reptiles in Snake Park and the exotic birds in the Tropical House to the dolphins and seals in the Oceanarium, there is plenty to keep you entertained in between outings to the beach.

Addo Elephant National Park

Situated some 72 km (45 miles) north of Port Elizabeth, this small national park was gazetted in 1934 to protect the last 11 Cape elephants resident in the area. The elephant population today stands at around 100, while other wildlife includes black rhino, buffalo, eland, the delightful ground squirrel, and 150 bird species. A good road network emanates from the rest camp at the main entrance gate. Close to Addo, the exclusive Shamwari Game Reserve is centred on a restored colonial farmhouse; guided game drives in open vehicles usually sight lion, elephant, rhino and antelope. 49

Apple Express

If you're nostalgic for the days of steam, climb aboard the Apple Express. The narrow-gauge line links Port Elizabeth with the town of Loerie via the superb country-side of the fruit-growing Lang-kloof Valley.

Graaff Reinet

Some 270 km (170 miles) north-west of Port Elizabeth, Graaff Reinet, founded in 1786, is the fourth-oldest European settle-ment in South Africa. The old town preserves 220 buildings and private dwellings, most of them listed as national monuments. They include Cape Dutch houses, Karoo flat-roofed cottages, Victo-rian villas, and a striking Dutch Reformed church modelled on Salisbury Cathedral. The town is in the centre of a region of widely scattered farmsteads. Merino sheep and angora goats graze the sparse vegetation; rainfall is uncertain and summer temperatures can reach 40 °C (104 °F).

Bordering Graaff Reinet, the Karoo Nature Reserve embraces over 40,000 acres of rare plant-life, as well as zebra, antelope and wildebeest. Also within the park are the cathedral-like rock forma-tions of the Valley of Desolation.

Mountain Zebra National Park

Near Cradock, a lively agricul-tural centre on the banks of the Great Fish River, the park was gazetted in 1937 to ensure the survival of the Cape mountain zebra, a race endemic to South Africa. Some 200 of these rare creatures roam the reserve, which is also home to red hartebeest, black wildebeest, springbok, and more than 200 species of birds. On the northern slopes of the Bankberg chain at an altitude of 2,000 m (6,600 ft), the park offers stunning panoramas of the Karoo.

THE XHOSAS

The Eastern Cape is the home of the Xhosas, second in number only to the Zulus among South Africa's tribal groups. They have spread far beyond this province, especially to the cities, and provided many of the political leaders who campaigned against apartheid, includ-ing Nelson Mandela. In rural areas, the Xhosas live in thatched, cir-cular huts called rondavels and wear woollen scarves as turbans. The women often paint their faces with ochre and smoke long pipes; young unmarried men may be seen with their faces painted ghostly white. The Xhosa language with its characteristic clicking sounds and range of tones is easily recognized but hard to learn.

► NORTHERN CAPE

Upington, Kuruman, Augrabies Falls National Park,
Kgalagadi Transfrontier Park, Namaqualand,
Richtersveld National Park, Kimberley

Bordered by Botswana and Namibia to the north, the Free State to the east and the Atlantic Ocean to the west, the Northern Cape is the largest province in South Africa, and the most sparsely settled, supporting a mere two percent of the national population. Arid, wild, in part desert, the region is off the tourist track, probably because of its distance from the big cities. Nevertheless, it is easily accessible and contains some of the most beautiful countryside in South Africa, several nature reserves, four major national parks, and a diamond town way over to the east on the Free State border.

Upington

This is the main travel lynchpin of the Northern Cape and the obvious springboard for visits to the region's national parks. Straddling the banks of the Orange River (the country's largest waterway), it's an attractive and welcoming town, though quite small, with an excellent local history museum attached to the tourist information office.

Upington's legendary Le Must ranks as one of the finest traditional Cape restaurants in the entire country, while the Orange River Wine Co-op (reputedly the largest wine co-operative in the world) produces an array of drinkable and reasonably priced plonks.

TAKE THE "A" TRAIN

Several companies offer luxury on rails. The Blue Train travels in style between Cape Town and Pretoria, three times a week in each direction, with a special extension to Victoria Falls in Zimbabwe six times a year. Rovos Rail runs from Cape Town through Kimberley to Pretoria and Victoria Falls every week, through Knysna on the Garden Route every two weeks, with occasional special excursions to Lusaka (Zambia) and Dar-es-Salaam in Tanzania. Historic steam locomotives are used where possible, and some of the carriages are 100 years old. The Union Limited makes rail safaris of up to 15 days, around the western and northern Cape and the Garden Route, stopping to allow trips to the sights along the way.

The Spitskop Nature Reserve on the outskirts of Upington harbours herds of gemsbok and springbok. In Keimos, 40 km (25 miles) further east, the Tierberg Nature Reserve consists of a steep hill swathed in spectral kokerbooms and colourful aloes, and affords memorable views over the Orange River and associated agricultural scheme.

Kuruman

Ideally situated to break up the long drive between Gauteng and Upington, Kuruman is arguably the most attractive town in the Northern Cape, centred on a tree-lined natural spring—The Eye—that yields more than 50,000 cubic litres of freshwater daily.

About 6 km (4 miles) north of town, the Kuruman Mission founded in 1821 by the Scots missionary Robert Moffat—with its stone buildings and shady orchards—has the aura of a misplaced English country church surrounded by arid semi-desert. The Kuruman Mission was Livingstone's first posting in Africa, and a plaque commemorates the tree under which he proposed to Moffat's daughter Mary, before they were wed in the mission church.

Erosion in the Augrabies Park has formed a gorge 240 m deep.

Two worthwhile attractions lie within easy day-tripping distance of Kuruman. The Wonderwerk Cave, on the Danielskuil Road, has sheltered humans for millennia, and contains the earliest evidence of people using fire, as well as some defaced rock paintings. The Witsand Nature Reserve is named for a series of white dunes that stand in bold contrast the surrounding red dunes—it's also a magnificently remote spot enlivened by the chorus calls of jackals and hyenas by night.

Augrabies Falls National Park

About 120 km (75 miles) west of Upington, the waters of the Orange River plunge from a height of 56 m (184 ft) into a deep granite gorge to form the spectacular Augrabies Falls. The noise of the churning wall of water against the rock inspired the Khoikhoi to give the falls the name Augrabies, which in their tongue means "deafening". Look out for the colourful agama and Cape flat lizards that scamper around the rocks above the waterfall.

Well-equipped with a camping area and bungalows, this national park is primarily of scenic interest, though it is populated by leopard, eland, rhinoceros, baboon, antelope and springbok. Hikers and strollers can take advantage of bountiful possibili- 53

The gemsbok, or oryx, can easily withstand the rigours of the Kalahari desert.

ties here, while night drives in an open vehicle offer a good chance of encountering a variety of nocturnal predators such as serval, caracal and genet. More adventurously, the Augrabies Rush is a half-day rafting trip that passes over a succession of grade 1 to 3 rapids upriver of the waterfall.

Kgalagadi Transfrontier Park

Slightly more than 200 km (120 miles) north of Upington by road, the former Kalahari Gemsbok National Park penetrates into the vast Kalahari Desert. The last refuge of the San, the desert also covers parts of Namibia and Bo-

tswana. The park, founded in 1931, originally covered 9,500 sq km (3,700 sq miles), making it the second largest in the country after the Kruger Park. In 2000, it was amalgamated with Botswana's Mabuasehube-Gemsbok National Park to form the co-managed Kgalagadi Transfrontier Park—at 38,000 sq km (14,800 sq miles) one of the largest protected wilderness areas in the world.

A mesmerizing landscape of tall red dunes, overhung by a seemingly permanent blue sky, and transected by the Auob and Nossob Rivers (neither of which flow more often than once in ten years), this vast, arid park would be worth the admission price for its austere scenery alone. But it also happens to offer superb game viewing: lion, leopard, cheetah, spotted hyena, bat-eared fox and black-backed jackal are all like to be seen over the course of a few day's visit, while more elusive nocturnal predators include the aardwolf and brown hyena. The handsome gemsbok (oryx) for which the park was originally named is common, as are spring-bok, eland and wildebeest. The appealing ground squirrel, meerkat and yellow mongoose thrive on the dunes, as does an excellent selection of dry-country birds and raptors.

Remote as it is, the Kgalagadi park is easily reached and explored in an ordinary saloon car, and three rest camps—Twee Rivieren, Mata Mata and Nossob—provide comfortable accommodation and a range of provisions.

Namaqualand

From the end of August until the end of September, after the southern hemisphere's springtime rains, the normally arid and inhospitable plains of Namaqualand—a succulent-rich region dividing the Western Cape from the Kalahari—are transformed into an immense carpet of some 4,000 species of vividly coloured flower. The small country town of Springbok, about 300 km (186 miles) west of Upington, is a popular and well-equipped base from which to explore the floral displays, as—closer to Cape Town—is the underrated West Coast National Park near Suldhana Bay.

Richtersveld National Park

Further north, near the border with Namibia, Richtersveld National Park continues nature's festival. Among its rocky mountains and immense sandy plains, half of the plant life found here is unique to this part of the world. The Half-mens (or Elephant's Trunk) trees, with trunks crowned by a clump of leaves resembling a human head, count among the most astonishing plants on earth.

Temperatures in summer can be extremely hot, but you can share the cool of the evening with the desert-loving springbok. Rise at dawn to drive along dry river beds and you may see a family of cheetah silhouetted against the skyline.

Kimberley

The capital of the Northern Cape, the legendary diamond town of Kimberley, on the border with Free State, is sure to interest anyone dazzled by sparklers. Four mines, made up of a labyrinth of galleries, own the lion's share of the glittering prizes.

The vast Kalahari desert is formed by rolling dunes of windblown copper-red sand.

The Kimberley Big Hole is the biggest man-made crater in the world. Since 1869 almost 28 million tons of "blue ground" have been shifted to obtain three tons of diamonds. The hole, now a waterlogged depression, covers an area of 27 acres. More than 30,000 miners worked here during the last century. The site and its surroundings, which you can reach on the Kimberley tram from City Hall, have been converted into an open-air museum where 50 or so cottages, shops, offices, pubs and churches have been scrupulously reconstructed as they would have appeared at the height of the diamond rush.

While you're here, visit the San (Bushman) Cultural Project, a living exhibition of the artefacts and way of life of an almost vanished people. Also worth an hour or two is the Duggan-Cronin Gallery on Egerton Road, which houses an illuminating collection of photographs of rural Africa taken all around the continent in the 1930s.

Further afield, Driekopseiland, 70 km (43 miles) from the town centre, is the site of over 3500 ancient rock engravings on exposed basement rock in the bed of the Riet River. Unlike other sites, the drawings here are 90 per cent geometric in design.

To many South Africans, the Western Cape is the most beautiful and most varied of all the South African provinces. This fertile countryside, washed on either side by the Indian and Atlantic oceans, like the Cape of Good Hope itself, was the place where the European history of South Africa began.

Cape Town

Surrounded by attractive and fashionable beaches, Cape Town is one of the most enticing cities in the world. It was founded in 1652 by Jan Van Riebeek to provide a port where the ships of the Dutch East India Company could take on supplies on their voyage east. The setting, at the centre of exceptional sites of natural and cultural interest, couldn't be more spectacular. At the foot of the legendary Table Mountain, with ocean waves breaking on its shores, Cape Town's old colonial houses rub shoulders with dizzying skyscrapers.

Parliament

The Houses of Parliament, seat of legislative power in South Africa, are on Government Avenue. They also house a historical museum, an art collection and memorabilia of the first Cape parliament from 1854. The avenue runs alongside what were once the fruit and vegetable gardens of the Dutch East India Company, part of which have been converted into a splendid botanical garden.

City Hall

On Darling Street, City Hall is built in an architectural style at once reminiscent of the Italian Renaissance and British colonial times. This remarkable building of 1905 is used today as a concert hall and for occasional special ceremonies. It is set off by a huge esplanade, where a lively market is held daily.

Castle of Good Hope

Built in 1666, the castle is one of the oldest European constructions in southern Africa. In the form of a five-pointed star, this fortress has never been under siege and owes its celebrity to the men of note who were imprisoned within its walls. The main attractions are the Ceremony of the Keys, which takes place at 10 a.m., and the Changing of the Guard, at noon. The guided tour includes the torture chambers and cells; it will make you wonder how they came to call the castle "Good Hope".   57

Museums

Cape Town's many museums cover every aspect of culture. The Jewish Museum, on Hatfield Street in the oldest synagogue in the country, has a good collection of ceremonial art and recounts the history of the Jewish communities of the Cape. Nearby, the South African National Gallery has a permanent collection of works by both national and international artists. The South African Museum in Queen Victoria Street is the most venerable museum in the country, with an international reputation founded on its natural history department. It is worth a visit for the anthropology section and planetarium alone. The Museum of Cultural History in Wale Street at the junction with Upper Adderley Street occupies what was a house for slaves built in 1679 by the Dutch East India Company. Highlights are its collections of arms and coinage and the archaeology section.

The maritime history of the Cape of Good Hope is retold in the South African Maritime Museum, Dock Road, Cape Town Harbour, with a handsome collection of model ships.

Bo-Kaap

At the foot of Signal Hill, the brightly coloured dwellings of the Bo-Kaap ("above the Cape") district are inhabited by the descendants of Malay slaves who were brought here during the Dutch occupation. It remains a staunchly Islamic community. The earliest mosque of the Cape, the Jamia Mosque (1850), stands at Chiappini and Castle streets and illustrates, along with the Bo-Kaap Museum, the Islamic culture of the area.

Historic Monuments

Begin with the pretty Victorian houses of Long Street, where antique dealers and booksellers abound and the South African Association of Arts displays the works of contemporary South African artists. The Groote Kerk, the oldest church in the country (1704), has a wooden pulpit sculpted by Anton Anreith and a fine collection of Cape silver.

Victoria and Alfred Waterfront

The old port of Cape Town has had a facelift. Prince Alfred, son of Queen Victoria, laid the foundation stone of these basins and quays in 1860. The area is now a focal point attracting the Cape's young crowd day and night. Tourists, of course, are carried along with the throng.

A short distance from the city centre, the reinvigorated Victoria and Alfred Waterfront is the general rendezvous spot, where you can stroll, shop or enjoy a good

The Cape painted in the soft colours of sunset.

meal—fresh fish and seafood are specialities. Here, too, are museums, theatres, a brewery, hotels, luxury boutiques and a huge shopping centre. This is also the place to book boat trips and helicopter flights over the surrounding region.

Beaches

The nearest beach to the city centre, Sea Point is a densely populated area with tall apartment buildings and hotels facing many small sandy coves. Clifton is more spacious and is popular with the young and fashionable, while nudists take it all off at Sandy Bay, to the south.

Robben Island

North of Table Bay, 5 km (3 miles) offshore, lies the notorious former prison island where Nelson Mandela and numerous other political prisoners were held for almost 20 years. Now you can take a tour to see the grim little quarters where the convicts lived, and the quarries where they chipped stone.

Table Mountain

In fine weather, a cable car will carry you up to the top of Table Mountain in seven minutes—the hike up (safer with a guide) takes about two hours. From the summit, at an altitude of 1,087 m 59

CAPE PENINSULA

(3,570 ft), you can survey one of the finest panoramas in all South Africa—inspiration to meander among the wild flowers on one of the walks and climbs adapted to all levels of ability. Common mammals on the mountain include the rock hyrax (which looks rather like a grey guinea pig) and troops of habituated baboons.

Constantia

On the eastern slopes of Table Mountain, the Kirstenbosch Botanical Gardens display 4,000 of the 18,000 plant species which have been classified in South Africa, including 2,600 natives of the Cape Peninsula.

Groot Constantia, the country's oldest established vineyard, now a state-owned experimental farm, surrounds a superb 17th-century manor house in Dutch gabled style. This has been converted into a museum, furnished with antique pieces of the period. The paintings and porcelain are particularly fine.

Cape Peninsula

Extending 50 km (31 miles) south from Cape Town, the Cape Peninsula is a scenic feast of tree-covered mountain slopes and a dramatic coastline of soaring cliffs, rocky bays and lagoons. The best beaches are at the northern end, with warmer waters on the east side facing False Bay. The road round the peninsula stays close to the sea wherever it can, revealing a succession of superb views. Chapman's Peak Drive, cut into the rock face above Hout Bay, is one of the highlights.

Hout Bay

The best harbour on the west side of the peninsula is the home of a fishing fleet. Mariner's Wharf on the quay is the place to buy rock lobsters (crayfish), live or ready cooked, or to dine in one of the restaurants. Artists have moved into some of the old houses and others are used as holiday homes.

Cape of Good Hope

The most southerly landfall of Africa is Cape Agulhas, 150 km (94 miles) to the southeast. But both historically and touristically Bartolomeu Dias's Cape of Storms, renamed Good Hope by John II of Portugal, remains the focal point of an astonishing region and an obligatory pilgrimage for every visitor.

Nature Reserve

In the Cape of Good Hope Nature Reserve, established in 1939, almost 2,500 varieties of flowers bloom between and on the rocks. Here you will see the delicate marsh rose, a member of the family of proteaceae that has so far resisted all attempts to cultivate it. Every spring, the Cape Peninsula celebrates the wedding of the cold waters of the Atlantic with the warm eastern seas amidst a terrestrial ocean of flowers. Surrounded by these splendours, ostrich, baboon and bontebok cavort in complete freedom.

Simon's Town

Once a British naval base, this port is now the headquarters of the South African Navy, whose frigates share the harbour with countless pleasure craft. Ashore, you can see the 1740 Admiralty building. A 1790 Martello Tower houses the Naval Museum. A popular nearby attraction is Boulders Beach, where a 3,000 strong breeding colony of penguin fusses, squawks and waddles around like an army of hysterical black-tie waiters.

Fish Hoek

With a fine safe beach for swimming, Fish Hoek on the more sheltered east side of the peninsula is a popular resort with local families and Europeans fleeing the northern winter. It is unique in South Africa being "dry"; bars and liquor stores were banned when land was granted to build the town in the 19th century.

Muizenburg

The fast inland highway from Cape Town brings city dwellers in their thousands to the holiday 61

retreats along Muizenburg Bay, the start of an amazing 35-km (22-mile) stretch of wide sandy beach. Many people from Johannesburg have second homes here.

Hermanus

The quaint town of Hermanus—all cobbled alleys and creaky Victorian buildings—is an old whaling station perched dramatically below the cliffs of Walker Bay, about 80 km (50 miles) east of Cape Town as the crow flies. The cliffs form a spectacular vantage point for whale watching, most reliably from June to late October, when Southern Right Whales migrate here from Antarctica to breed.

Wine Country

The charming university town of Stellenbosch, founded by Simon van der Stel in 1679, is the second oldest settlement in the country, situated on the banks of the Eerste (First) River about an hour's drive inland of Cape Town. Distinguished by its shady oak-lined avenues, Stellenbosch hosts what is probably the greatest concentration of Cape Dutch gabled homes in the country, a highlight

South African wines are heady and very drinkable. Get to know them better by tasting at all the houses along the wine route.

being the so-called Village Museum, a block of restored 18th century buildings entered from Ryneveld Road.

Stellenbosch is the principal town of the Cape Winelands. Some 30 major vineyards, several established in the 17th century, operate in the immediate vicinity of the town, and most can be visited for impromptu tasting sessions along the renowned Stellenbosch Wine Route. One of the most beautiful—and highly regarded—wine estates in the region, with a memorable setting beneath tall purple crags, is Boschendal, centred on a stately Cape Dutch building and reached via an avenue of tall trees.

North of Stellenbosch, Paarl, named for a pearl-like rock formation overlooking the town, is the headquarters of the giant KWV wine co-operative, and boasts more than its share of historic buildings. Tullbagh, further north still, has the finest assembly of Cape Dutch houses, restored twice—before and again after an earthquake in 1969. Nearby Ceres is the Cape's fruit capital, surrounded by apricot, apple and pear orchards. Worcester's grapes, grown within sight of winter snows, form the basis of South Africa's best brandy.

Arguably the loveliest of the vineyard villages is Franschhoek, or "French Corner", where French 63

Huguenot refugees settled after fleeing religious persecution in France in 1688, bringing along their wine production skills. Set in a magnificent green valley a short distance east of Stellenbosch, this small village hosts a clutch of great restaurants and worthwhile museum dedicated to the history of the Huguenots. Of several less celebrated wine-producing areas, the Robertson Valley—slopes lined with almost 30 different estates—is well worth exploring. Even the more established vineyards in this region (Robertson Winery, Van Loweren, De Wets Hof) are seldom visited by large tours, so the atmosphere at tasting sessions is less production line than it is around Stellenbosch. What's more, assuming that you're thinking of buying, the Robertson vineyards generally represent great value for money.

Garden Route

From the Western Cape to the Eastern, a narrow strip of land between the coast and the mountains concentrates so much variety and scenic beauty that it has become South Africa's most popular holiday destination.

Swellendam

The most significant urban punctuation along the N2 as it runs east from Cape Town towards the Garden Route is Swellendam, founded in 1743, making it the third-oldest town in the country. A blazing fire in 1869 destroyed many of the town's older buildings, but the old Drostdy, built four years after the town was founded, today doubles as a local history museum and tourist information office. The underrated Bontebok National Park, only 6 km (4 miles) from the town centre, was founded in 1930 to preserve a herd of endemic bontebok, and it also protects Cape mountain zebra, red hartebeest and a good selection of birds.

Cape Agulhas and Elim

About 100 km (60 miles) south of Swellendam, Cape Agulhas is the most southerly point in Africa, a desolate stretch of rocky coastline that has claimed at least 250 ships since the 17th century. A lighthouse built in 1848 is a national monument. One of the most picturesque villages in South Africa, Elim consists of a cluster of 19th century fishing cottages about an hour's drive west of Agulhas.

Mossel Bay

If you are coming from Cape Town, your introduction to the Garden Route will start at Mossel Bay, where the Portuguese ex-

Along the Garden Route, the wild flowers form a carpet of colour.

plorer Dias came ashore in 1488. His landing is the inspiration for the local historic and maritime museum, the Bartolomeu Dias Museum Complex. In the park above the beach stands an ancient milkwood tree where sailors used to leave messages to be relayed by other ships. There is now an official letterbox where you can mail home cards, which will be franked "Post Office Tree".

From Mossel Bay, there are sailings to Seal Island where a colony of 2,000 seals lives in the middle of a bird sanctuary, principally for Cape gannets and cormorants. The small town has also become something of a focal point for adventure activities, including bungee jumping at the nearby Gouritz Bridge, sea kayaking, and caged dives to look for great white sharks.

George

Founded in 1811 and named after George III of England, this pleasant, leafy town stands a little inland, 60 km (40 miles) east of Mossel Bay. A steam train rather preciously named the Outeniqua Choo-Tjoe runs all the way to Knysna. The three-hour journey is well worth taking as it's the only way to see some of the most spectacular countryside of the Garden Route.

At the station, an old container depot has been converted into the Outeniqua Railway Museum which, besides ancient locomotives, displays road transport vehicles and toy train sets.

Wilderness

On the Knysna road, the forest-fringed, freshwater lakes and lagoons of Wilderness National Park make an enchanting spot for birdwatching (fish eagles and waders); fishermen and water-sport enthusiasts congregate in the tranquil resort of Wilderness.

Knysna

A British colonist, George Rex, rumoured to be the illegitimate son of George III, settled here some 20 years before the official founding of Knysna in 1825. Nature-lovers never fail to be impressed by the pink rocks of The Heads and the Knysna National Area. Stinkwood and yellow-wood trees grow in the forest carpeting the slopes of the Outeniqua Mountains; ancient specimens can be seen in the Garden of Eden near Plettenberg Bay. But Knysna's claim to fame is the size and succulence of its oysters—oyster-and-champagne sunset cruises run daily from the waterfront.

Adventure activities in the vicinity of Knysna—bookable through the tourist information office—include abseiling, diving, mountain bike trails, and canoeing up the river.

The Diepwalle State Forest, north of Knysna, protects the last three truly wild elephants in the Western Cape.

Plettenberg Bay

This most opulent of the Garden Route resorts boasts three pretty beaches and has a huge selection of accommodation options suited to all budgets.

The Robberg Nature Reserve, 10 km (6 miles) out of town, protects a craggy peninsula covered by a 10-km walking trail. Seals and humpbacked whales are occasionally seen from the cliffs of Robberg, and a variety of seabirds—notably a breeding colony of the handsome black oystercatcher—is guaranteed.

Totally different in character, the Keurbooms River Nature Reserve, 4 km (2.5 miles) out of town, protects a stretch of the river fringed by lush forest teeming with small mammals and birds, and best explored along an overnight canoe trail.

Tsitsikamma Coastal National Park

Protecting an 80-km (50-mile) stretch of rugged coastline east of Plettenberg Bay, this national park is perhaps best-known as the site of the country's most famous hike, the magnificent Otter Trail, which is often booked solid a year in advance. A taster of what this trail offers is provided by day walks out of the Storms River rest camp, which lies near the breathtaking cliffs that enclose the Storms River Mouth. The residential village of Nature's Valley, at the western edge of the reserve, is surrounded by coastal forest running down to a lovely, calm beach.

The Tsitsikamma Forest National Park is noted for several podocarpus conifers more than 300 years old.

Cape St Francis

Further east towards Port Elizabeth, the resort of Oyster Bay lies on one of the most beautiful beaches of this stretch. Along the shore near Cape St Francis, sea otters can be observed; the marine nature reserve is also a refuge for seals. Jeffrey's Bay, richly scattered with shells, is a paradise for surfers. The season starts in March.

Oudtshoorn

The detour inland to Oudtshoorn, about 60 km (38 miles) to the north of George, is highly recommended. You can visit the Cango Caves (27 km, 17 miles further north) with their stunning stalactites and stalagmites, see a crocodile ranch, and spend time at an ostrich farm. Thanks to the 19th-century fashion craze for ostrich feathers, several farmers of the region built immense stately homes, which became known as feather palaces. These are open to visitors, with guided tours and ostrich shows. The gangly birds, ridden by jockeys, take part in races which you can enjoy while tucking in to ostrich steaks.

Karoo National Park

It is well worth extending your journey by 200 km (125 miles) further north to Beaufort West, in the semi-desert plain of the Western Karoo. The town has a Dutch Reformed Church in the Gothic style, a museum in the old Town Hall, an old Mission Church and Manse. But the detour is chiefly justified by the Karoo National Park, offering an explosion of flowers every spring, as well as abundant game and a chance to spot the blue crane, South Africa's national bird. A unique feature of this park is a walking trail that concentrates on the region's rich variety of fossils.

West Coast

North of Cape Town on the West Coast, the Lobster Road leads to the holiday resort of Strandfontein. Birds and birdwatchers alike flock to the West Coast National Park, one of the biggest marshlands in the world and home to some 55,000 feathered friends in summer: cormorants, Cape gannets, sandpipers, gulls, plovers and pink flamingoes.

There's a pleasant beach at the Langebaan Lagoon near Churchhaven; the busy port of Saldanha is known for its old thatched cottages. The nearby islands are colonized by seals, penguins and Cape gannets. The area around Langebaan often becomes a riot of colour in spring—the Postberg Nature Reserve sometimes hosts some of the most spectacular floral displays in the country.

At Lambert's Bay, the gannet colony roosts on a peninsula close to the port, along with a small flock of resident penguins. The history of the region is recounted at the Sandveld Museum.

Vineyards and Orchards

A succession of beaches and fishing harbours are strung along the coast. Inland, the vast orange groves of Citrusdal on the Olifants River produce 2 million crates of citrus fruit every year. One of the farms boasts the oldest orange tree in Africa. The valley also produces wine.

Further to the east, the Cedarberg Mountains have weathered into natural sculptures of golden sandstone. Many outdoors lovers regard this spectacular range to be the finest hiking areas in South Africa, and it also boasts some wonderful rock art and spring wildflower displays. The Kagga Kamma Reserve is home to a small community of San people.

Shopping

Take a measure of African mystery, a taste of the Orient, blend with typically Western luxury and you have the recipe for shopping in South Africa—as eclectic as the population. In a word, there is something for everyone.

Keep the original invoices for items you intend to export. You can then obtain a refund of the VAT (sales tax) from customs offices at ports and airports of departure from South Africa. You may have to show the goods to the customs inspectors so don't pack them away.

African Tribal Art

The numerous cultures which make up South Africa have given birth to a colourful and lively tradition of craftsmanship, perpetuated for the greater happiness of the shopping-prone tourist. What with masks, spears, shields, sculpture, paintings, pottery and multicoloured bead necklaces, the choice is staggering.

Gems

Diamonds are virtually synonymous with South Africa, one of the principal producers with 24 per cent of world reserves. Don't forget, however, that the finest diamonds are cut in Amsterdam and Antwerp. Their value is determined by the world market price, which is dominated by De Beers. If you buy diamond jewellery, be sure to ask for an official certificate of provenance, with a full description of each stone. There is a wide selection of semi-precious gemstones, uncut or cut and mounted.

Gold

Gold may be bought for a little less than elsewhere, but be sure that you are getting 18 carat gold, as 9 carat is widespread in shops throughout the country.

Ostrich leather

For a souvenir which is both practical and attractive, choose leather goods in ostrich skin. Characterized by its bumpy surface, ostrich skin is incredibly tough and hardwearing. Conservationists needn't worry: the skins come from ostrich farms which are mainly situated 69

Nama women adopted patchwork techniques and voluminous dresses from the missionaries of Victorian days.

around Oudtshoorn. If you feel more daring, you can also buy plumes for your Easter bonnet or your feather boa. Briefcases, handbags, wallets, shoes, belts, even jackets and coats make welcome gifts. The finest-quality leather is exported to Italy, where it is made into elegant fashion items before being sent back to South Africa to grace the smartest boutiques. There is also a wide range of goods in farmed buffalo and crocodile skin.

And More...
If your friends are all hoping for a small souvenir of your South African journey, bear in mind the woven mats, painted ostrich eggs, Indian spices, and protea flowers. Another idea is one of the better Cape wines, brandies or citrus-flavoured liqueurs.

Anything to Declare?
Preferably before going to South Africa, and certainly before you leave, find out what imports are banned in your own country. Otherwise you may face an unpleasant surprise on your return home—having your souvenirs confiscated (not to mention a fine). Most western countries have signed the Washington convention aiming to protect endangered animal and plant species.

Sports

Many South Africans are fanatical about fitness. Weekends are dedicated to the outdoor life; you'll see countless runners and cyclists as well as a mass migration to the beaches. There's a boom in adventure sports, from ballooning to bungee-jumping, river-rafting, mountaineering and horseback safaris. In spectator sports, return to world competition has proved South Africa's rugby, cricket and soccer teams to be top class.

Water Sports

The endless beaches stretching along South Africa's 3,000-km (1,900-mile) shoreline are a permanent inducement to swim and take part in all kinds of popular water sports, including windsurfing, water-skiing, scuba diving and surfing (for which the Wild Coast south of Port Edward is particularly good).

But watch out for the sharks and mind the tides—swim only at beaches that are marked safe. Some beaches have lifeguards on duty. In addition, most hotels have swimming pools. Inland, canoeing and rafting are available on every navigable river or stream.

South Africans are also enthusiastic sailors. In practically every port and at most waterside leisure centres you can try your hand at sailing, whatever your degree of competence.

Fishing

Fishing is popular on the high seas and in rivers (you can obtain a licence in the towns or villages near to the stretch of water you hope to fish). The catch is particularly abundant near Cape Town, where the Indian and Atlantic oceans meet.

Deep-sea fishing expeditions are organized for tourists on a regular basis, leaving from all the big ports, principally from the Cape between January and April and from Durban between June and November along the KwaZulu/Natal coast.

Walking

The Blyde River Canyon Reserve in Mpumalanga and the Drakensberg Mountains are excellent places for walking or hiking through in unspoilt countryside. A network of pathways has been

South Africa offers opportunities for all kinds of sports from abseiling to white-water rafting.

laid out between the most attractive sites of some national parks and circuits adapted to horse-riding or to mountain-biking are also marked.

Spectator Sports

Athletics has a large following in South Africa, and many competitions are organized both outdoors and indoors. Rugby is practically a religion among the white population, cricket of course has its enthusiasts, and football (soccer), is the favourite sport of the black people—the national team is one of the best in Africa.

Fans of motor racing flock to the track at Kyalami, north of Johannesburg, even though the South African Formula 1 Grand Prix has not been held for several years.

Tennis

Most large hotels have their own tennis facilities and visitors will have no difficulty in finding a court.

Golf

Such is the popularity of golf that the country sometimes gives the impression of being one immense golf course. There are almost 500 official courses and visitors are welcomed everywhere, generally at prices lower than in Europe.

Dining Out

Rich agricultural lands, a livestock tradition which includes sheep, goats, cattle and poultry, and a privileged geographical situation have brought South Africa fresh produce of the highest quality: fruit, vegetables, meat, fish and seafood. And don't forget the wines of the Cape, which have a worldwide reputation for excellence. Rich, healthy and abundant, South African cooking tends to be good, plain, unsophisticated food prepared in the American style, but with borrowings from Britain, India and Southeast Asia.

Meat

Barbecues, or *braaivleis*, are a South African institution and constitute the favourite weekend meals for family gatherings—rather like a picnic in your own garden. Indeed, most picnic sites and camping grounds are provided with barbecue pits, so that all you need is some meat or fish and a bag of charcoal to provide the basis for a pleasant Sunday in the open air.

Some South African specialities to try are *bredie*, mutton stew flavoured with tomato sauce; *boerewors*, sausages spiced with cinnamon; and biltong, air-dried beef, ostrich or antelope meat, usually served as a starter. Eaten mostly around the Cape, *bobotie* is curried minced meat with onions and eggs, baked.

Seafood

Fish and shellfish of all kinds figure largely on the menus of restaurants along the East Coast and around the Cape. Absolutely delicious and affordable in price, lobster is very good value, so spoil yourself. Oysters, shrimps and mussels make their appearance on magnificent seafood platters and the staggering variety of fish will tempt you to new culinary experiences: try *kingklip*, *kabeljou* or *snoek*.

Alternatives

If you begin to tire of barbecues and fish, then most towns of any size will have several restaurants offering Asian or European cuisine to tempt your jaded palate. Durban is noted for its Indian restaurants. Johannesburg and

White, red or rosé, South African wines are definitely worth investigating.

Cape Town have a great variety of international cuisines, and fast-food restaurants are springing up everywhere.

Increased interest in traditional ways means that adventurous eaters can test their courage. At African cultural evenings you may be offered samples of local "bush tucker" such as fried locusts, termites and beetle grubs, or dried worms.

Wine

South African wines have made up for the lost time of apartheid and international boycotts, improving in quality and range. They are generally labelled by grape variety. Cabernet Sauvignon, Hermitage (Cinsault), Shiraz and Pinotage, a hybrid of the pinot noir wines of Burgundy and the Hermitage of the Rhone, are among the best reds. Connoisseurs of Bordeaux wines will especially appreciate the excellent Meerlust. Chardonnay, riesling, sauvignon and chenin blanc make reliable whites.

There are some good rosés, reminiscent of light Swiss wines. The great variety of their soils explains the diversity of the Cape vintages.

One of the delights of South Africa is eating lunch or dinner among the vineyards and tasting the local wines on the spot.

The Hard Facts

To help you plan your trip, here are some of the practical details you should know about South Africa

Airports

The major international gateway is Johannesburg (also serving Pretoria), but an increasing number of international carriers now fly directly to Durban and Cape Town from Europe, America and Asia. All three airports have every facility required by today's traveller, including travel and car-hire agencies and duty-free shops.

Airport buses run to city centres, and some hotels operate their own shuttles.

Climate

South Africa is, for many, practically synonymous with sunny skies, and in most parts of the country it is unusual indeed to experience persistent overcast weather. South of the equator seasons are the inverse of those in the northern hemisphere: the winter solstice (the shortest day) comes in June and the summer solstice (the longest day) in December. The main rainy season in is summer (November to April), when dramatic but short-lived afternoon thundershowers are to be expected every few days. The exception is the Western Cape, where most of the rain falls in winter (June to August). In the interior, the climate is generally drier in the west, with parts of the Kalahari and Karoo falling into the semi-desert bracket.

Local and seasonal climatic conditions vary considerably. The Cape Town area has a temperate, Mediterranean climate, while the coast of KwaZulu-Natal and the Kruger National Park enjoy permanent sub-tropical conditions. The high plateau around Johannesburg is generally warm to hot in summer but is often surprisingly chilly at night, with temperatures dropping below zero in winter. The Drakensberg can be very cold in winter—some areas regularly receive snow.

Winter is a good time if you are planning a photographic safari.

Clothing

Pack clothing suitable for a hot temperate climate. In summer, it is advisable to include a light sweater for cooler evenings, especially if you are visiting the mountain regions or the south of 75 the country. In winter, a couple of heavier sweaters will probably be required. You may need a raincoat if you are visiting the Cape in winter. The usual style is relaxed and casual, with sports clothes very much in vogue especially in the mountains and the nature reserves. If you are planning to stay in luxury hotels or dine in high-class restaurants, more formal attire will be required.

There's no need to dress up like a professional ranger when you visit a game park, but the brown or beige of the traditional safari suit has its merits. Drab colours are less likely to disturb the animals. In the open vehicles used in private parks, wear a hat, sunglasses and plenty of sunscreen. At night, long sleeves, long trousers and socks help to fend off mosquitoes.

Communications

At the main post offices, you pay for your telephone calls at the counter, but otherwise you will need a pocketful of change if you phone overseas from a callbox, which can swallow coins at an amazing rate. Nevertheless, this is much cheaper than calling from your hotel room, where the charges are frequently doubled. Green callboxes accept phonecards, available for 10 to 200 rand. Direct dialling is the norm. Cellular phones are in widespread use.

Check with your service provider to see if yours is compatible. Fax machines are widely available, and most hotels of any quality now offer internet and e-mail services.

Consulates

There are foreign consulates in Pretoria, Cape Town, Johannesburg and Durban. The local yellow pages of telephone directories list them under "Consulates and Embassies".

Driving

The main roads are excellent, and even the unsurfaced roads in national parks are usually quite smooth. Driving is on the left, as in Britain. Tolls are charged on some major roads. The general speed limit is 120 kph (75 mph) on motorways and marked sections of main roads away from towns where traffic is light. Elsewhere it is 100 kph (62 mph). In populated areas it is 60 kph (37 mph) unless otherwise posted. Radar traps are common and seat belts must be worn. An international driving licence is required unless your national licence carries your photograph.

Members of automobile clubs can pick up free brochures and maps at South African AA offices in the big cities on presenting their membership cards. Petrol stations are reliably open from 7 a.m. to 7 p.m., but many operate 24 hours a day. Petrol is cheap by comparison to most parts of Europe, but note that it cannot generally be paid for with a credit card—you'll need cash. Away from towns, they can be far apart, so it's advisable to fill up whenever you can.

Avoid driving at night or alone. Plan routes in advance, and seek local advice about safety. In the cities, close car windows and lock doors. This makes air-conditioning essential, and it's useful too in the game parks and on dusty roads where you need to keep windows shut. Park in well-lit places, guarded if possible, and leave nothing on show.

Electricity

The current is 220/250 volts AC, 50 cycles. Plugs have three round pins. Bathroom plugs for razors, hairdryers and nickel-cadmium battery chargers have two pins.

Emergencies

To call the police, the number is the same everywhere in South Africa: 1-0111. To call an ambulance, dial 1-0177.

Formalities

Tourists from the European Union do not in general need a visa for South Africa, but must show their return ticket. A valid passport is obligatory.

Non-resident tourists can import duty free all their personal effects, and gifts and new articles to a value of 500 rand. Visitors over 16 can import 400 cigarettes, 50 cigars and 250 g tobacco, 1 litre spirits (liquor), 2 litres wine, 50 ml perfume and 250 ml toilet water.

Health

Standards of hygiene are very high and there is no risk involved in drinking the tap water in your hotel or in eating fruit or vegetables, no matter where you are staying. Hospitals and medical services are of a good standard, but treatment must be paid for. In an emergency you will find a list of doctors in the telephone directory under Medical practitioners.

Avoid swimming in stagnant water (bilharzia is endemic) and be aware of the dangers of malaria in the lowveld of Mpumalanga, Zululand and Swaziland (which basically means any beach or game reserve north of Durban and east of the escarpment). Consult your doctor and start your course of anti-malarial tablets before leaving home, and carry them with you. Use insect repellent, and try not to get bitten. As for any journey abroad, it is advisable to take out a health insurance policy covering illness and accident while on holiday.

Hours

Banks generally open Monday to Friday 9 a.m. to 3.30 p.m. Some 77 branches open also on Saturday mornings 8.30 a.m. to 11 a.m. Shops generally open Monday to Friday 8.30 a.m.–5 p.m., and on Saturdays 8.30 a.m.–12.30 p.m. Post offices are open weekdays 8.30 a.m.–4.30 p.m. and Saturdays 8 a.m.–noon.

Languages
The eleven official languages are Zulu, Xhosa, South Sotho, North Sotho, Ndebele, Venda, Tswana, Shangaan, Swazi, English and Afrikaans. English is spoken in all hotels, and as in many other parts of the world it is the main language in the tourist centres.

Media
The many daily newspapers published in English cover all the local, national and international news. The South African Broadcasting Corporation (SABC) has 24 radio channels broadcasting in 17 languages and 3 television channels in 7 languages. A fourth public channel called etv broadcasts chiefly in English, as does the cable network M-Net/DSTV.

Money
The South African unit of currency is the rand (R), which is subdivided into 100 cents. Banknotes are issued in denominations of 10, 20, 50, 100 and 200 rand, and coins are 1, 2, 5, 10, 20 and 50 cents as well as 1, 2 and 5 rand.

Most credit cards and travellers cheques are accepted in hotels, restaurants and shops, but not in petrol stations.

Cash machines (ATMs) outside banks will generally issue cash against most internationally recognized credit cards, but beware of pickpockets and muggers who watch these sites.

Public Holidays
When a public holiday falls on a Sunday, the Monday is taken off. These are the official public holidays:

January 1	New Year's Day
March 21	Human Rights Day
March/April	Good Friday and Easter Monday
April 27	Constitution Day
May 1	Labour Day
June 16	Youth Day
August 9	National Women's Day
September 24	South Africa Day
December 16	Reconciliation Day
December 25	Christmas Day
December 26	Charity Day

Public Transport
The best way to cover the vast distances in South Africa is by air. Several airlines serve the principal towns and cities. The railway network offers moderately priced travel in sleeping cars to

most parts of the country. There are also several long-distance coach companies. An excellent hop-on, hop-off minibus service called the Baz Bus, which connects Johannesburg to Cape Town via Swaziland, KwaZulu Natal and the Eastern Cape, is used extensively by most backpackers.

Taxis cannot be hailed on the street, but must be ordered by telephone or hired from pick-up points. Insist on having the meter switched on; if there isn't one, agree a price in advance.

Safety

By staying alert and taking sensible precautions, you should be able to avoid problems. When going out in the cities at night, travel in a group, and take a taxi to and from the restaurant, theatre or wherever you are spending the evening. Do not walk alone at night, or at any time in less-frequented places, including beaches. Don't wear or carry valuables, expensive watches or "real" jewellery. Use the security devices on hotel doors. Leave no property unattended.

Time

GMT + 2 all year round.

Tipping

Restaurant bills do not include a service charge. Tip about 10 percent of the total bill. Porters and taxi drivers also expect a tip.

Toilets

Cleanliness—sometimes even luxury—is guaranteed in all large hotels and restaurants. Most public toilets maintain an acceptable standard.

Tourist Offices

To obtain useful brochures and maps before you leave home, contact Satour, the South African Tourism Board.
UK:
   5–6 Alt Grove
   London SW19 4DZ
   tel. (020) 8971 9350
USA:
   Suite 2040
   500 Fifth Avenue
   New York, NY 10110
   Tel. (212) 730 2929
   e-mail: satourny@aol.com
Canada:
   Suite 205
   4117 Lawrence Ave. E,
   Scarborough, Ont. M1E 2S2
   Tel. (416) 283 0563

Website www.southafrica.net

INDEX

GENERAL EDITOR
   Barbara Ender-Jones
REVISED EDITION
   Philip Briggs
LAYOUT
   Karin Palazzolo
   Alain Piccard
PHOTO CREDITS
   Ariadne van Zandbergen:
   pp. 2, 5, 7, 9, 19, 25, 27, 29,
   35, 52, 70 , 72, 74;
   B. Joliat: pp. 17, 21, 22, 23,
   32, 43;
   Hémisphères/Lechenet:
   pp. 14, 62, 65
   Hémisphères/Guignard: p. 40
   R. Cavassini: pp. 54, 56, 59
MAPS
   Elsner & Schichor;
   JPM Publications

Copyright © 2003, 1999
   by JPM Publications S.A.
   12, avenue William-Fraisse,
   1006 Lausanne, Switzerland
   information@jpmguides.com
   http://www.jpmguides.com/

Printed in Switzerland
Weber/Bienne (CTP) — 03/05/01
Edition 2003–2004

SWAZILAND

African Kingdom

Enclosed on three sides by South Africa, and bordering Mozambique to the west, the Kingdom of Swaziland is one of Africa's smallest nations—less extensive than the Kruger National Park—and its only surviving absolute monarchy. Strong economic ties to South Africa—epitomized by an interchangeable currency and the ubiquitous South African chain stores—might sometimes lead one to think of Swaziland as a tenth province of that country in all but name. Yet, you only have to scratch beneath the surface to discover it has a quite distinctive character, determined by the cultural resilience of its rural inhabitants and their proud adherence to traditional ways.

Seldom visited as a stand-alone travel destination, Swaziland forms a natural extension to a tour through South Africa—indeed, for anyone driving between the popular Kruger National Park and KwaZulu-Natal, it will be easier and more rewarding to traverse the kingdom than to pass around it. The Swazi, as a rule, are charming hosts, and scenically, the kingdom is magnificent, with the misty mountain landscapes of the western escarpment standing in compelling contrast to the sweltering acacia bush of the Mozambique border region.

Tourists generally restrict their time in Swaziland to a quick flit through, punctuated perhaps by an overnight stop. But a burgeoning selection of new sites and activities justifies a longer stay. Swazi cultural villages offer fascinating insight into traditional African lifestyles, while a clutch of low-key game reserves is noteworthy for providing the rare opportunity to track the highly endangered rhinoceros on foot. Adventure activities, too, have become a Swaziland trademark, ranging from horseback safaris and self-guided game walks to white-water rafting, abseiling and rock climbing.

A Brief History

Pre-1800	Swaziland's history is similar to that of South Africa. In 1750, King Ngwane, regarded as founder of Swazi Nation, arrives in the area.
19th century	Centralization under King Sobhuza I, whose army, forged in defence against the militant Zulu, conquers an area twice as large as modern Swaziland. Outsiders come to know this kingdom as Swazi, a corruption of the name of Sobhuza's successor Mswati II. From 1850, the Swazi regu-

larly side with settlers against rival Zulu and Pedi, in the process being persuaded to sign one-sided treaties sacrificing parts of the kingdom for vain promises of protection. In 1894, with tacit British approval, Kruger's Transvaal Republic claims protectorateship over Swaziland. The incumbent King Bhunu doesn't accept Boer presence, and his power is reduced to such an extent that he is tried for murder.

20th century   Boer rule is terminated in 1902 during the aftermath of the Anglo-Boer War, when Swaziland becomes a British protectorate separately administered from South Africa. King Sobhuza II (rules 1921–82) places continual pressure on the British government to accord greater rights to his subjects, resulting in about half of the protectorate being designated as communal Swazi land in 1944. Sobhuza peacefully leads his nation to independence in 1968. Shortly afterwards, he revokes the Westminster style constitution in favour of one based on traditional lines—effectively outlawing opposition parties and granting the king almost absolute power. In 1986, Mswati III ascends the Swazi throne, and is still in power today.

Sightseeing

Northern Highlands

Coming from the Kruger Park, the normal point of entry is the **Jeppe's Reef/Matsamo** border, where—in the no-man's land between immigration offices—it's well worth stopping at the **Matsamo Cultural Village**. In addition to a great coffee shop overlooking a pond stocked with crocodiles, Matsamo offers informative guided tours through a Swazi village, traditional dancing, and visits to a *sangoma* (traditional healer).

Set in rolling hills 40 km (25 miles) south of the border, the sleepy former mining town of **Piggs Peak** (founded 1884 by William Pigg) boasts a few banks and supermarkets, but is of little inherent interest to visitors. However, 10 km (6 miles) back along the Matsamo road lies the popular hotel and casino named after the town, as well as the attractive **Phophonyane Nature Reserve**. Privately owned and serviced by a cluster of chalets, this compact reserve is centred on an impressive waterfall, while a network of foot trails through its wooded 83 slopes offers an opportunity to see several small mammals and a selection of colourful forest birds.

South of Piggs Peak, **Malolotja Nature Reserve** is the most beautiful sanctuary in Swaziland, protecting a vast landscape of hills and valleys spanning an altitude range of 640–1,829 m (2,100–6,000 ft). Some big game is present, most visibly zebra, red hartebeest and blesbok, but Malolotja is of greater interest for its unusual flora—endemic species of cycad, protea and aloe—and as a breeding site for the rare bald ibis and blue swallow. A limited road network exists, but essentially Malolotja is the domain of pedestrians: a steep but scenic half-day round hike leads to the 90-m (295-ft) Majolomba Falls (the tallest in Swaziland), and overnight trails of up to five nights in duration are also available.

South of the entrance gate to Malolotja, the road from Matsamo connects with the main road between Mbabane and the **Oshoek/Ngwenya** border post (the normal point of entry coming from Gauteng). Two very different sites of interest lie close to the road between the junction and the border. The Ngwenya Glass Factory is a unique set-up that makes and sells a wide selection of artefacts—glasses, candleholders and miniature animals—using recycled glass. More enduring in nature is **Ngwenya Mine** (a southern extension of Malolotja), the oldest known working in the world, dated to 41,000 BC, when its haematite and specularite deposits were used for ritual and decorative purposes.

The West

Sprawling over a pretty green valley in the western highlands, **Mbabane**, the national capital, with a population of about 50,000, has a rather provincial atmosphere, and—shopping malls and a few consulates aside—there's little to distinguish it from a hundred other medium-sized Southern African towns. Founded in the 1880s, Mbabane's temperate climate made it attractive to British settlers and it became capital of the protectorate in 1903—contemporary photographs indicate it then consisted of about a dozen stone buildings. A pretty Cape Dutch building on Allister Miller Street was the first British administrative office.

A short drive north of Mbabane leads to the steep, smooth slopes of **Sibebe Rock**, reputedly the largest exposed granite dome in the world, the tip of a solid chunk of granite (or batholith) that extends 15 km (9 miles) below the earth's surface. Reminiscent of Australia's famous Ayers Rock—which is larger, but composed of sandstone—Sibebe can

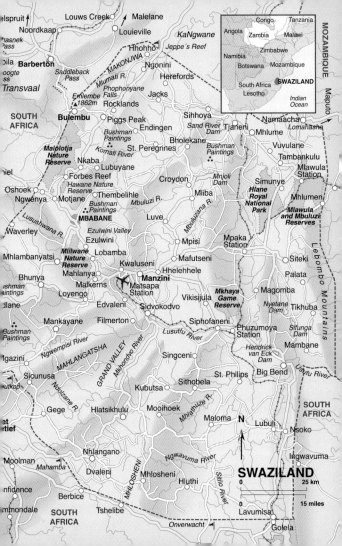

be ascended over a couple of hours in the company of an experienced local guide.

A spectacular—and in misty conditions treacherous—asphalt road winds southwest from Mbabane through the wooded **Ezulwini Valley**, the hub of Swaziland's tourist industry. The valley is serviced by several plush hotels, many of which started life in the apartheid era, when Swaziland attracted white South Africans eager to indulge in activities—gambling and liaising with black prostitutes—that were illegal at home. A vibrant nightlife remains a feature of the valley—some hotels still double as casinos or strip clubs—but the main focus today is a selection of more wholesome natural and cultural sites.

The indigenous scrub of the **Mantenga Nature Reserve**, situated in the heart of the valley, supports a riot of colourful birds, while monkeys frequent the woodland near a pretty waterfall. The centrepiece is a cultural village where visitors can watch vibrant dancing displays accompanied by virtuoso traditional musicians. The village is overlooked by the Execution Rock—from where, in pre-colonial times, convicted murderers were thrown to their death. At the turn-off to Mantenga, Swazi Trails operates a range of adventure activities out of Ezulwini, most popularly **white-water rafting** trips on a nearby stretch of the Great Usutu River studded with Grade I–IV rapids.

Lobamba, at the south of Ezulwini Valley, is the traditional seat of the Swazi monarchy, and the site of national parliament. The informative **National Museum of Swaziland** at Lobamba houses several displays relating to the royal lineage, a fascinating collection of photographs from the early 19th century, and a more prosaic natural history room full of musty stuffed animals. The adjacent **King Sobhuza II Memorial Park** pays tribute to the popular ruler who secured Swaziland's independence from Britain, and is where his body was laid in state prior to a traditional burial in the hills.

Also in the Ezulwini Valley, **Mlilwane Nature Reserve** is the kingdom's oldest sanctuary, converted from private farmland and donated to a non-profit trust in 1969. Ecologically compromised by several stands of exotic eucalyptus, Mlilwane has nevertheless made a vital contribution to conservation in Swaziland. Hippopotamus wallow in a pool at the rest camp, while reintroduced zebra, warthog and antelope—including blue wildebeest, nyala, blesbok and impala—are common. A noteworthy feature of Mlilwane is that you can walk unguided along an extensive network of foot trails, or explore on horseback.

Roughly 40 km (25 miles) southeast of Mbabane, the road through Ezulwini emerges at **Manzini**, the kingdom's largest town and industrial hub. Founded in 1889 as Bremersdorp, Manzini served as the capital of Swaziland before being usurped by Mbabane. Although not overly endowed with character, it is of interest for its bustling central market—an excellent place to buy traditional handicrafts—and on Thursday host to a macabre traditional medicine market.

The Lowveld
Climatically and scenically, eastern Swaziland resembles bordering low-lying parts of Mpumalanga and KwaZulu-Natal, and it supports several vast sugar plantations around Simunye and Big Bend. The country's main concentration of game reserves also lies in the eastern lowveld, and while none exists on the scale of the Kruger Park, all are worth exploring. Swaziland's wildlife showpiece is **Hlane Royal National Park**, a 3,000-hectare tract of bush originally set aside as the royal hunting ground, and still visited on ceremonial occasions by King Mswati III to pot an antelope. The rest camp at the entrance gate overlooks a waterhole that attracts a steady trickle of game.

Self-drive roads offer perhaps the highest probability in Southern Africa of encountering white rhino, while elephant, black rhino, greater kudu and nyala are regularly seen. Lions and cheetahs are housed in large natural enclosures that can be visited only with escorted trips in four-wheel drive vehicles arranged at the rest camp. An exciting feature of Hlane is the inexpensive guided walks that run through an area teeming with rhinos and elephants.

East of Hlane, a trio of contiguous reserves protects the lushly wooded slopes of the Lubombo Mountains and associated river valleys. **Mbuluzi** and **Mlawula Nature Reserves** both protect giraffe, zebra, various antelope, and an excellent range of birds, and since no dangerous large mammals are present, they can be explored on foot. By contrast, **Shewula Community Reserve**, unique within Swaziland in that it's owned and managed by a local community, is primarily a cultural centre: local village visits and other cultural activities are run out of a clifftop rest camp offering spectacular views in three directions.

Further south, the dense acacia woodland of **Mkhaya Game Reserve** was set aside in 1979 to protect Swaziland's last surviving herd of pure Nguni cattle, a breed with high resistance to diseases that can kill exotic caws. Mkhaya 87 also hosts introduced breeding herds of locally endangered game species such as sable and roan antelope. Dense populations of both Africa's rhino species, as well as elephant, are easily observed. Mkhaya is too small to support large predators without a risk of them attacking local livestock, but leopard spoor is occasionally seen.

Shopping

Many curios and handicrafts sold in South Africa are imported from Swaziland, and it's cheaper—and healthier for the local economy—to buy at source. The glass factory at Ngwenya is well worth a visit, as is the renowned candle factory in the Ezulwini Valley. The produce of both can be bought at curio shops and stalls all countrywide, as can a wide selection of Swazi basketry, beadwork and carvings.

Well-stocked supermarkets are found in all major centres, but the selection of goods in smaller towns is limited.

Practical Information

In most respects, what is true for South Africa holds true for Swaziland. Exceptions are noted below.

Credit cards. Most hotels, restaurants and larger shops accept credit cards, but ATMs issuing cash against credit cards exist only in Piggs Peak, Ezulwini, Mbabane and Manzini.

Currency. The Swazi Lilangeni (plural Emalangeni) is pegged to the South African Rand. The two currencies are interchangeable within Swaziland, but not within South Africa—so don't leave Swaziland with excess Emalangeni.

Driving. South African vehicles entering Swaziland must pay a nominal insurance fee at the border. Be wary of animals and pedestrians running unexpectedly into the road.

Language. The official languages are Swazi and English, the latter generally spoken to a high standard.

NAMIBIA

Diamonds and Dunes

Elephants and lions prowl Namibia's greatest national park, but things get even more exotic. From magnificent red-gold sand dunes to a diamond-studded mineral bonanza land, from the gloomily named Skeleton Coast to the time-warp architecture of the towns, Africa's youngest independent country is clearly somewhere very different. Local radio stations speak a dozen languages, but in practice all you have to know is English, German or Afrikaans.

Namibia, formerly known as Southwest Africa, has only been independent since 1990. Before that it was ruled from South Africa, but for three decades at the turn of the 20th century it was a German colony. The Kaiser's era left a lasting mark on the urban landscape—and on the gastronomic traditions, which are still heartily inclined toward sausages and sauerkraut and plenty of beer. *Karneval* and *Oktoberfest* are the year's biggest festivals at Windhoek, the colourful upland capital.

Sparsely populated, Namibia is about three-fourths the area of South Africa, or ten times the size of Austria. It is bordered on the west by the South Atlantic, on the south by South Africa, on the east by Botswana and on the north, by Angola. And a bit of gerrymandering, the narrow panhandle of the Caprivi Strip, extends Namibia's frontier like a barbed spear into Zambia and to the tip of Zimbabwe.

Getting around is easy—the extensive highway network is in good shape. For long distances, domestic flights might be more convenient; even for sightseeing trips, nothing can compare with a flight over the dunes.

In the rainbow of races united under the blue, green, red and gold Namibian flag, members of tribes linked under the Ovambo name account for about half the population of 1.6 million. The Kabango, Herero and Damara people are the next numerous, and white Namibians are estimated to total 90,000. The population of Bushmen, or San, handsome hunter-gatherers as featured in the film, *The Gods Must Be Crazy,* has dwindled to a few tens of thousands. About 90 percent of all Namibians profess Christianity, with the Lutherans easily in first place.

The treacherous coast stretches for about 1,400 km (more than 800 miles), yet there is only one proper deepwater port, Walvis Bay, long a strategic enclave of South Africa. Inland there is still plenty of room for antelope and zebra, giraffe and hippo, and sights that can only be seen in the heart of Africa.

A Brief History

Prehistory	Rock art, pottery and tools show that prehistoric hunter-gatherers lived in Namibia. The early inhabitants are thought to have been Khoisan speakers, including San (Bushmen) and Khoikhoi, or Nama, people.
15th century	Portuguese explorer Diego Cão marks his visit to Cape Cross by erecting a cross on the shore. His countryman, Bartolomeu Diaz, "discovers" Walvis Bay, but finding no fresh water he abandons thoughts of colonization.
18th century	In 1793 the Dutch claim Walvis Bay. But Britain soon annexes South Africa's Cape Colony (1795) and claims the adjoining Namibian coast.
19th century	First German missionary station opened at Bethanie in 1814. German missionaries fan out through the territory in mid-century. They ask Britain for protection but this is refused. Britain annexes Walvis Bay in 1878. A Bremen merchant, Adolf Lüderitz, buys the small port of Angra Pequena in 1883 and raises the German flag over what is to become the town of Lüderitz. In the 1880s and 1890s German settlers occupy other parts of South West Africa, signing treaties with native tribes. Swakopmund is founded in 1893 by Captain Curt von François and 120 German colonial troops. At the turn of the 20th century Herero tribesmen and Germans engage in years of bloody battles. The well-armed Germans win.
20th century	In 1908, Germans discover the world's richest diamond bonanza in the southern zone of South West Africa; prospectors flood in.
	In World War I, on behalf of the Allies, South African forces capture South West Africa from Germany. "Undesirable" German settlers and military personnel are expelled. South Africa rules under a 1920 League of Nations mandate, much contested in the decades ahead. When the United Nations succeeds the League of Nations after World War II, South Africa refuses to put South West Africa under UN trusteeship. The South West African People's Organization (Swapo) is established in 1958 to resist South African rule and apartheid. In 1966 Swapo launches

a guerrilla war for independence. After UN-supervised elections, Africa's last colony, Namibia, becomes an independent nation in 1990. Its first president is Sam Nujoma, leader of Swapo, who pushes for national reconciliation. In 1993 South Africa hands over Walvis Bay sovereignty to Namibia.

Sightseeing

The tourist authorities divide Namibia into four regions: Northern, Central, Southern and Namib. These are arbitrary delineations that have nothing to do with provincial boundaries or other formalities. This guide follows the same format, starting in the central highlands, site of the nation's capital.

Windhoek

The compact skyscrapers of Windhoek oversee a prosperous city of more than 169,000 residents that's strong on individuality. The Germans who made this their colonial capital more than a century ago left a quaint legacy of Old World architecture, landscaping and lifestyle.

At an elevation of 1,650 m (5,400 ft), the capital is largely immune to the swelter you might expect of Africa. Although the name literally means "windy corner", Windhoek has few blustery problems; the climate is refreshing with plenty of rain to keep the lush gardens and flowerbeds well watered.

As dynamic as the skyscrapers may be, it's the low-rise monuments from colonial days that win on charm. Start with the **Alte Feste**, an old whitewashed fort designed by Curt von François in 1890. Its severity is relieved by palm trees and gardens. The oldest structure in town now houses part of the state museum, dealing with many aspects of Namibian history and culture from tribal times to independence.

The Parliament building, dating from late in the German era, owes its curious nickname of **Tintenpalast** (Ink Palace) to the reams of edicts and reports penned by the bureaucrats on duty inside.

The **Christuskirche** (Church of Christ) was built in the same period as the Tintenpalast, at the turn of the 20th century, to give thanks for the end of wars between the Germans and local tribes. This Evangelical Lutheran church, a neo-Gothic building with a slender tower, rises gracefully in native sandstone. The stained-glass windows were a gift from Kaiser Wilhelm II.

Modern architecture tops the expanding skyline of the Namibian capital, Windhoek, but the colonial era buildings are preserved.

The architecture on the main street, **Independence Avenue** (formerly Kaiserstrasse), is a lively contrast between the steep, overhanging red roofs of the Germanic tradition and new international-style highrises. Strolling and shopping are rewarding. Take a break at an outdoor café, where the beer, too, recalls old Germany, but the passers-by represent a brilliant medley of European and African cultures.

Central Excursions

Local colour, charm and cleanliness commend Windhoek to the visitor. The capital is also a good base for excursions. For instance, less than half an hour's drive takes you to the **Daan Viljoen Game Park**, where you can start your checklist of African wild animals you've spotted. You'll get close to highland game animals like springbok and mountain zebra, hartebeest and eland (Africa's largest antelope). There are no lions or other dangerous animals so the park is a safe place to travel on foot; just follow the marked trails. And the bird-watching is first-class.

The **Von Bach Dam and Recreation Resort**, in the mountains north of Windhoek, is a favourite getaway spot for the capital's sportsmen, especially anglers. The dam positively wriggles with carp, bream and black bass.

The highway and the railway line for the coast veer west at the 93

attractive and historic town of **Okahandja**, the old capital of the Hereros, about 70 km (40 miles) north of Windhoek. Every year (in August) crowds of colourfully dressed participants gather for a memorial service to honour the Herero chiefs buried here. And here, too, is the tomb of Chief Jonker Afrikaner, originally an arch-foe of the Hereros. The town's church, now a national monument, was built in the 1870s, after the foundation of a mission station.

Just southwest of Okahandja, Namibians and foreigners "take the waters" in a luxurious hot spring resort on the site of a historic mission station. It's called **Gross-Barmen**, based on the name of the town the German missionaries came from in the 1840s. The ruins of the mission and an army camp remain. The natural springs here produce water rich in fluorides and sulphides, which bubbles out of the ground too hot to bathe in. It has to be cooled for use in the thermal baths and further cooled for the outdoor swimming pool, which is not exactly chilly, either.

The junction town of **Karibib**, west of Okahandja, owes its prosperity to the railway, a mission station and, last but not least, a nearby gold mine. The earth is truly generous here: fine marble of international renown is quarried in the area, and there are reserves of gemstones.

Omaruru, on the way to the Etosha National Park, has a violent history. The Germans established a police post here, and it was besieged by the Hereros in a brutal war in 1904, with heavy losses. A museum documents the Herero War and the tragic battle of Omaruru.

Mountain scenery and Stone Age culture are the attractions of the **Erongo Mountains**. The best-known site is the Phillips Cave, in which a Stone Age wall-painting of an elephant shows remarkable detail.

More rock paintings are found near the **Spitzkoppe**, a family of granite peaks (advertised as the "Matterhorn of Namibia") rising suddenly from the plain. Because of the setting the mountains appear taller than they really are (around 1,800 m or 5,900 ft).

North of Omaruru, the railway tracks go through the village of Kalkfeld, but what makes the area famous are **dinosaur tracks**. The footprints, thought to be more than 150 million years old, are now a national monument.

The next stop on the railway is the junction town of **Otjiwarongo**, a prosperous market centre. Wildlife enthusiasts can visit the local Crocodile Ranch.

Moving from reptiles, and up a mountain, you can see some fas- 95 cinating game roaming **Waterberg Plateau Park**. This national park encompasses most of the fertile, flat top of a mountain rising dramatically east of Otjiwarongo. Endangered species were given priority in populating the surprisingly lush landscape. Among those prospering here are white and black rhino, roan and sable antelope, giraffe, cheetah, and a highly prized colony of rare vultures. The Waterberg is also known for its rock paintings and engravings.

Strange geological sights are a speciality of the Damaraland region, west of Otjiwarongo. Looking as tall as a skyscraper, **Vingerklip** ("rock finger") is a bizarre outcrop, a limestone monolith left over from centuries of erosion. It's 35 m (115 ft) high.

The fossils of tree trunks thought to be 200 million years old and amazingly well-preserved are the phenomenon of the **Petrified Forest**, a national monument near Khorixas. Geologists believe the trees were uprooted from a forest far away and carried here by a sort of biblical flood.

Near the Petrified Forest, at **Twyfelfontein**, is one of Africa's greatest concentrations of rock art. Thousands of primitive paintings and engravings deal with the concerns of Stone Age hunter-gatherers—pictures of lions, elephants, giraffes and rhinos. The artists may have come this way thousands of years ago.

And one more geological wonder: near the **Burnt Mountain** (a study in desolation), slabs of basalt stand like a surreal skyscraper skyline. They are called the **Organ Pipes**, and they're probably more than 100 million years old.

The South

The pleasant town known as the "capital of the south", **Keetmanshoop**, was founded by German missionaries in the 1860s. The former mission church, built in 1895, houses a museum of colonial memories and ethnological exhibits. Farmers in the Keetmanshoop area raise karakul sheep for their wool and fur (known in some circles as Persian lamb, but the Namibian variant is called Swakara). The dry, hot climate here agrees with the animals, natives of Central Asia.

The arid land just northeast of Keetmanshoop also supports hundreds of strange botanical specimens in the **Kokerboom** (Quiver Tree) **Forest**. Quiver trees are not technically trees at all, but giant aloes resembling parched, peeling dragon trees. They grow to a height of 8 m (more than 25 ft).

Namibia's version of the Grand Canyon, the **Fish River Canyon**, is a ravine that is up to 27 km (17 miles) wide and in places more than 500 m (1,600 ft) deep. At the bottom of this spectacular gorge, the river itself is a bit of an anticlimax—a trickle at best, except at flood time.

Ai-Ais (the name means scalding hot) is a spa in the wilderness of the canyon. You'll find the hot springs at the heart of a thoroughly modern resort complex with facilities for all sorts of therapeutic endeavours as well as rest and recreation.

For history buffs the village of **Bethanie** holds a certain allure. This is where the German colonial powers signed the first treaty with the Hottentots. In Bethanie stands the country's oldest European house, a one-room cottage called Schmelenhaus after the missionary Heinrich Schmelen.

In the Kokerboom Forest, northeast of Keetmanshoop, the major botanical attraction is the Quiver Tree—really a giant aloe.

GEISTERSTADT

For sheer, desperate melancholy it's hard to beat the ghost town of Kolmanskop, just southeast of Lüderitz. Wind-blown sandhills have all but submerged some of the houses, though others have been restored to keep alive the memory of boom times in the hunt for diamonds in *Südwestafrika*. No one has lived in Kolmanskop since the 1950s. Photographers love it.

Namib Region

The sleepy town of Lüderitz was the first German port in South West Africa, but its history can be traced back to a visit by the 15th-century Portuguese explorer Bartolomeu Diaz. The fanciful German architecture from the first decade of the 20th century adds charm to the romantic setting.

The **Namib-Naukluft Park**, the biggest national park of Namibia and one of the biggest wildlife preserves in the world, encompasses a staggering array of scenery, from mountains to grasslands to a desert of titanic dunes. The inhabitants are just as varied—mountain zebra, springbok, ostriches, and birds that can fly, such as eagles and falcons. The park covers an area of nearly 50,000 sq km (more than 19,000 sq miles), the size of New Hampshire and Vermont together, or Sicily plus Sardinia. The desert reaches the most impressive dimensions in the central Sossusvlei area, reputed to have the tallest sand dunes in the world—piled up to heights of 300 m (nearly 1,000 ft). The desert supports more life than you may imagine: grasses, succulents and a unique prehistoric plant called *Welwitschia mirabilis,* which takes its moisture from the fog or dew.

Walvis Bay, the only deep-water port between Capetown and Angola, is a working port where freighters load up with Namibian minerals and trawlers feed the fish-processing factories. The production of sea salt accounts for the blinding white hills around the lagoon, made up of crystals evolving through evaporation.

Birdwatchers haunt the wetlands here for the spectacle of thousands of flamingoes and droves of other species, permanent residents or transients, thriving on the abundant seafood. Sea birds nest on giant "bird islands" offshore, built to exploit the value of their guano, which is exported most profitably as fertilizer.

The C14 highway heading inland from Walvis Bay soon enters the desert, providing a panorama of rolling dunes. Slidng down a steep sand hill is the sort of sport most visitors won't soon forget.

Holidaymakers from all over Namibia and abroad come to **Swakopmund**, across the river north of Walvis Bay. They savour its charm, its mild climate and attractive beach. This is a corner of old Germany on the South Atlantic, rich in architectural and other memories of the late 19th century when Captain von François and Dr Heinrich Göring (who would father the future *Reichsmarschall*) tried to stop tribal wars and build a colony.

Typical of the transplanted European atmosphere of the town, the former railway station (built in 1901) is solid and stately, with a steeple and verandahs, and palm trees to make it all seem out of joint. It has been refurbished as an elegant hotel in colonial style.

Other distinguished buildings of the era are scattered through the town: the Old District Courthouse, an Art Nouveau classic; the old gabled prison; and mansions like Woermann House, now serving as the public library, and Rittenburg, and the Hohenzollern House.

Near the beach, the Swakopmund Museum occupies the former Customs House. There are exhibits on the various indigenous cultures—weapons, artefacts, musical instruments and tools—as well as desert and ocean themes.

Visitors are often taken to admire a marvel of Industrial Revolution days, an 1896 steam locomotive nicknamed *Martin Luther*. The name is a wry reference to the engine's career—it was mostly broken down—and Luther's statement, "Here I stand…"

You don't have to go far out of town to experience the Namib desert (for which the region and the country are named). Some of it is the dune of your dreams, but much is a less glamorous rocky expanse. Here, too, is Rössing, a rare site for connoisseurs of industrial superlatives. This is called the largest open-cast uranium mine in the world, and visitors can watch the mechanical behemoths collecting the ore from this awesome hole in the ground.

Cape Cross, up the coast from Swakopmund, is the place where the first European explorer came ashore in these parts, and here Diego Cão planted a cross. Now the area is a **seal reserve**, the home of tens of thousands of Cape fur seals.

The **Skeleton Coast** has had its share of shipwrecks and other disasters, hence the forbidding name. The landscape is as varied as hypnotic dunes, rugged mountains and, of course, a beach that 99 goes on to infinity. Anglers land fish of inspiring proportions—blacktail, galjoen, kob and, perhaps less appealingly, shark.

Because of the hostile climate and terrain, the wildlife population ashore is rather skimpy, mostly antelope, jackal and ostrich. And rarest of all nowadays, the desert lion.

The North

In Namibia's most wonderful game park, the **Etosha National Park**, you can see lions, black rhino, elephants, giraffe, zebra and antelopes of many families. What brings the animals here is the Etosha Pan, a huge depression that is sometimes filled with rainwater. But around its periphery are springs that provide year-round refreshment for throngs of animals and birds. The mineral-rich springs also feed the grass, shrubs and trees in which the game like to hide.

Among the more gripping sights you may come across as you drive through the park: hyena, wildebeest, scaly anteater, and antelope including kudu, duiker, eland, gemsbok, and the tiny Damara dik-dik. Bird-watchers can try to chalk up some 325 species, as spectacular as the lilac-breasted roller and the crimson-breasted shrike; they make the average cardinal redbird look as pallid as a parish priest.

The area of the park has shrunk and expanded over the years, sometimes controversially, as the interests of farmers competed with wildlife preservation efforts. At last report Etosha covered 22,270 sq km (nearly 8,600 sq miles), which is bigger than Massachusetts, or more than half as large as Denmark.

Namutoni, near the eastern edge of the park, was the site of a small fort at the turn of the 20th century. A successor fort, long a ruin, was restored to its "Beau Geste" silhouette, declared a national monument, and turned into tourist accommodation.

DIRECT CURRENT

An oceanographic phenomenon called the Benguela Current takes the credit or blame for almost everything along the Namibian coast, from the wealth of fish to the prevalence of fog in autumn, winter and spring. Carrying some of the chill of Antarctica, the current causes rainfall to condense before it can go ashore, but the fog helps to make the desert bloom and provides drinking water for creatures large and small. The cold ocean also moderates the heat that would otherwise roast the countryside at these latitudes.

In Etosha National Park you can't miss the springboks. Everything, from elephants to giraffes, is on show, plus abundant bird life.

Okaukuejo, the administrative headquarters, has many tourist comforts and some dramatic entertainment: a floodlit water-hole where game can be admired at night. The third camp, **Halali**, with modern facilities, is located between the other two. All of them are open year-round.

East of the park, **Tsumeb** is a pleasantly shaded mining town, thriving on the basis of more than 184 different minerals found here. In addition to the minerals valuable to industry—silver, copper, lead and cadmium—the earth is a bonanza of gemstones and crystals, some of them on view in the local museum.

A final superlative: near the town of Grootfontein, the **Hoba Meteorite,** said to weigh 55 tons, is called the largest metal mete-orite on earth. It was discovered here in the 1920s but it probably arrived from outer space thou-sands of years ago.

In **Kaokoland**, near the town of Opuwo, the pastoral Himba people, numbering some 6000, are descendants of Herero herders who fled to the northwest when displaced by the Nama. The women are noted for their intri-cate hairstyles and jewellery of shell, copper and iron. Both men and women anoint their bodies with a cream made from rancid butterfat, ochre powder and an aromatic resin. This gives the skin a reddish sheen which corre-sponds to the Himba ideal of 101

beauty. They wear few clothes apart from a loin cloth or skirt of goat skin.

Dining Out

This is carnivore country, where the inviting aroma of an outdoor barbecue often fills the air. The local beef is good, but you might want to try something more specifically Namibian—venison or wild boar, for example, or even zebra. On the coast the accent easily switches from steaks and chops to fresh fish or seafood (for instance Lüderitz oysters and Namibian rock lobsters).

Thanks to the German connection, there are tasty sausages, salamis and smoked meats to be consumed with copious amounts of pickled cabbage (*sauerkraut*). They can be accompanied by an imaginative spectrum of breads and rolls, and followed by desserts (such as *Apfelstrudel* and *Schwarzwälder Kirschtorte*) so sumptuous they'll put your self-control at risk.

Two influences—German taste and the climate—coincide here to make beer drinking a popular pastime. The local beer is brewed according to grand old traditions formalized in the 16th century, but because of the hot climate the alcohol content is usually kept lower than the European equivalent.

South African wines, which include some first-class vintages, are also available.

They've been making Cape wine since the 17th century. The most popular grapes have traditionally been Cabernet Sauvignon. Mated with Pinot Noir this makes the popular Pinotage. Among the whites, look for Chardonnay and Sauvignon Blanc.

Shopping

The map of Namibia shows a swathe of the southwest marked, intriguingly, "Diamond Area 1 (Restricted Area)". Some of the baubles lying about there turn up in the shops—diamonds and semi-precious stones like topaz and tourmaline. And consider the hand-made jewellery with traditional African motifs.

Another Namibian speciality is fur. Karakul, a variety of Persian lamb, is fashioned into stylish garments under the Swakara name. Leather goods are interesting, though here the source may be buffalo or ostrich. Among native curios, look for dolls in Herero costumes, hand-carved tribal trinkets, Himba jewellery, pottery and basketwork.

On certain goods, such as jewellery, overseas visitors are exempt from the local sales tax.

A young Himba woman at her morning toilette.

Practical Information

Banks. Open Monday to Friday 9 a.m.–3.30 p.m., Saturdays until 11 a.m.

Clothing. In winter days are mild to warm, so you will need light summer clothes. But be prepared for chilly nights, even in summer.

Credit cards. Most shops, hotels, rest camps and restaurants accept internationally known credit cards.

Customs allowance. Travellers over 16 years of age may import duty-free 400 cigarettes and 50 cigars and 250 g of tobacco; 2 litres of wine and 1 litre of spirits; 50 ml of perfume and 250 ml of toilet water; other gift articles up to a value of N$50,000.

Currency. The Namibian dollar issued in notes of N$10 to N$200, and coins of N$1 and N$5. It has the same value as the South African rand, which is accepted as legal tender.

Driving. Namibia drives on the left. There is a general speed limit of 120 kph on open roads; reduce speed on gravel roads. Safety belts must be worn. Roads are clearly signposted. To hire a vehicle, you must be in possession of a valid international driver's licence. Cars and four-wheel-drive vehicles can be hired at Windhoek Airport and in Windhoek, Tsumeb, Walvis Bay and Swakopmund.

Electricity. 220/240 volts, 50 cycles AC. Plugs have three pins.

Health. Travellers to the northern parts of Namibia are advised to take anti-malaria precautions.

Language. English is the official language. German and Afrikaans are also widely spoken, and there are a dozen indigenous languages.

Telephone. To make an international call dial 09, then the country code (1 for Canada and US, 44 for UK), the area code and local number.

Tipping. It is usual to add a 10 per cent tip in restaurants.

Water. In the towns, the tap water is purified. In the countryside, some tap water, though fit for drinking, may taste salty.

BOTSWANA

Challenging Country

Luxury hotels and game lodges exist, but on the whole Botswana is a land of rugged, unspoiled wilderness. This is not a destination for the timid, what with the heat and the dust, and the chance of undisciplined elephants wandering into your path. The nearest filling station and water supply may be many miles away, and the road could deteriorate without warning from tar to gravel to sand.

But if you persevere, the sights are unique, uplifting, unforgettable. They include lonely landscapes as varied as deserts and lagoons, and dozens of species of wildlife from lions and leopards to giraffes and hippopotamuses. Hundreds of bird species are on show, and the reptiles range from dangerous snakes to dangerous crocodiles.

Botswana, formerly the British protectorate of Bechuanaland, covers an area bigger than France but slightly smaller than Texas. It is very thinly populated—about 1.3 million inhabitants—including nomadic San or Bushmen in the mysterious Kalahari desert, which spreads over more than half of the country. The majority of the population, overwhelmingly rural, clusters near the borders of South Africa and Zimbabwe. (Landlocked Botswana also shares a frontier with Namibia and touches Zambia at the confluence of the Zambezi and Chobe rivers in the north.)

Many other countries might well envy Botswana its democracy and strong economic growth. The republic's parliamentary system has worked well since independence was won—peacefully and uncomplicatedly—in 1966. The wealth came, heaven-sent, shortly afterwards, with the discovery of enormous diamond reserves. Until then the economy had been based on cattle-rearing, and livestock is still another tidy export earner. Botswana is, however, a rather expensive country for travellers.

The towns, starting with the capital, Gaborone, have points of interest but they're mainly staging posts for the big attractions—the 17 per cent of the country dedicated to preserving wildlife and nature in general.

Chobe National Park is the home of giant herds of elephant and buffalo, while Kgalagadi Transfrontier Park is the place to see lion and cheetah. The most unusual reserve is the Okavango Basin in the north, the earth's greatest inland river delta, surrounded by desert. The water attracts thirsty elephants, hippos, zebras and giraffes. You can explore it in a dugout canoe, but don't mistake a snoozing crocodile for a floating log.

A Brief History

25,000 BC	Stone Age ancestors of today's San ("Bushmen") and Khoe ("Hottentots") leave tools and wall paintings in Botswana.
1st–8th centuries AD	Bantu migration arrives from central Africa. Farming and mining communities develop.
14th century	Tswana clans (Batswana) of the Bantu people settle in the land.
19th century	Expansionist Zulu warriors threaten stability, setting off migrations of terrorized tribes in southern Africa. In 1820 the London Missionary Society sends Robert Moffat to convert the Batswana to Christianity. Later the Society's David Livingstone establishes a mission and converts many, including Chief Khama III. Gold is discovered near Francistown (1866). Alarmed at inroads of the Boers from South Africa, Khama asks for British protection. In 1885, to curb German influence in South West Africa and contain the Boers, Britain proclaims the protectorate of Bechuanaland. The capital is placed outside Bechuanaland, in nearby Mafeking, South Africa. Britain proposes giving Bechuanaland administration to the British South Africa Company, run by the tycoon Cecil Rhodes. Tribal chiefs go to London to plead for the status quo. Britain accedes but gives a strip of land to Rhodes for construction of his "Cape to Cairo" railway.
20th century	After Britain's victory in the Boer War, the Union of South Africa is established (1910). South Africa proposes to absorb Bechuanaland but tribal chiefs resist. Economic sanctions cut into exports. The British create an African Advisory Council in 1920, giving the Batswana a voice in the protectorate's government. Chief Khama III dies in 1923, aged 89. His son succeeds to the throne, but dies after only two years in power. The heir to the throne, Seretse Khama, is only four years old, so his uncle Tshekedi Khama takes over as regent. Studying law at Oxford, in 1948, Seretse Khama marries a white Englishwoman, Ruth Williams, touching off a crisis in Bechuanaland. The couple eventually arrive as private citizens.

107

Seretse Khama becomes leader of the Bechuanaland Democratic Party (BDP), which wins the first free legislative elections. Britain grants independence in 1966 and Sir Seretse Khama (knighted just in time) takes over the presidency of the new Republic of Botswana. Diamonds are discovered at Orapa, and the country becomes one of the world's top producers. Re-elected three times, Sir Seretse Khama dies in 1980. He is succeeded by Dr Quett Masire. The current president, since 1998, is Festus Mugae.

Sightseeing

The wilderness is beyond compare in Botswana, and there's plenty of it, but you have to start somewhere. We begin rather unromantically in the national capital, the destination for international flights.

Gaborone

Until independence, administrative power was south of the border in Mafeking, South Africa. Since then the new capital of Botswana, Gaborone, has grown rapidly and now counts more than one in ten of the nation's inhabitants. Expansion has been so drastic that the city is often dismissed as being characterless—just a modern sprawl around the financial and administrative centre.

Gaborone is mainly a transit point for the visitor rather than a sightseeing goal in itself. But while you're making plans, getting accustomed to the climate, changing money, and shopping along the nicely laid out Mall, you can take some time out to visit the **National Museum and Art Gallery**. The art is African and European, not just from Botswana. The museum provides a briefing on the Kalahari Desert, the lifestyle of its nomads, and the country's wildlife.

Serowe

Between Gaborone and Francistown, Serowe is Botswana's largest village, with a population of 60,000. It is also the home of the Khama royal family. A statue honours the first president of Botswana, Sir Seretse Khama, and the **Khama III museum** is devoted to the family's history in the 19th and 20th centuries. There are documents, uniforms and weapons. The museum, occupying the Red House, the family home, also has exhibits on the life of the local Bangwato people and the Bushmen.

If you're itching for more to see in Serowe, call in at the **nat-**

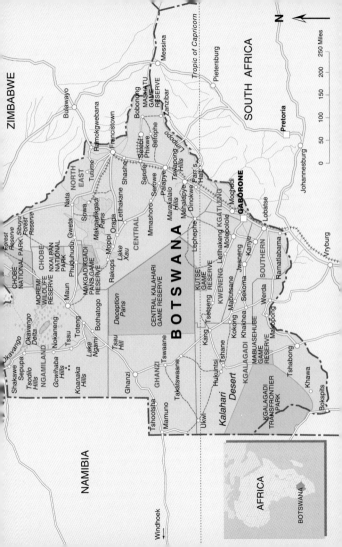

KALAHARI GLITTER

Serowe shares in the prosperity of Botswana's diamond rush. Hundreds of villagers are employed to process and polish some of the gems unearthed in the Kalahari. The first Botswana diamond field, discovered in 1967, was at Orapa, northwest of Serowe. But the biggest diamond mine was found in 1973 at Jwaneng, west of Gaborone. Security at the diamond sites is extremely vigilant; guided tours are not yet on the menu.

ural history museum, which includes more than a thousand species of insects.

Francistown

Linked to Gaborone by air, rail and a good road, Botswana's oldest city, Francistown, has been around since the gold rush of the 1860s. Most of the gold ran out, but not the less glamorous minerals, and the town was also able to keep going with agriculture and industry. Some atmospheric 19th-century buildings, like the old railway station, the jail and the courthouse, have been preserved. In the metropolis of the northeast you'll also find good hotels and shopping facilities, as well as a cinema.

Maun

Many safaris start in Maun, a Wild-West sort of town on the edge of the wondrous Okavango Delta. Its name means Place of the Black Reeds. The principal school of architecture here is the mud hut, to which some imaginative inhabitants have added extra interest by incorporating old soft-drink cans into the walls. Cattle wander freely along the dusty streets. So does a cast of characters ranging from authentic African villagers to expat tour guides, naturalists and hunters just back from the bush. Maun is the town for organizing a safari, or stocking up on provisions before setting forth, or sampling a few comforts of civilization after a tough time in the wilds.

National Parks

The animals and the birds, the scenery and the solitude are wonderfully preserved in Botswana's national parks and reserves. Accommodation ranges from the most lavish of lodges with en-suite bathrooms to spartan camp sites with the barest of necessities. But the nation's tourist policy aims to discourage crowds of backpackers in favour of a fairly limited number of big spenders, so you may have little choice but to wallow in luxury between excursions.

Safari camps provide great opportunities for getting close to the wildlife.

Gaborone Game Reserve

For tourists swooping in and out, the Gaborone Game Reserve, on the edge of the capital, gives a useful preview of some of the wildlife on show at the major national parks. Commuters from Gaborone can go out and back in a morning to see wildebeest, zebra, white rhino and several kinds of antelope. Early mornings and evenings are the best times for game spotting, but the reserve closes at 6.30 p.m.

Okavango Delta

Rivers always flow towards the sea, or try to, but the Okavango, which originates in Angola, is thwarted by geological fate. Unable to reach the Indian Ocean because of changes in the earth's crust, it spills into the sands of the Kalahari Desert, the most unlikely location for a vast delta system.

At the flood, the water swells to cover an area of more than 16,000 sq km (6,000 sq miles), much of it forming lagoons dotted with water lilies and shallow, narrow channels that are invaded by papyrus reeds.

All this clear, cool water attracts dozens of species of mammals, 200 of birds and 80 of fish, but the antelope, zebras and baboons are almost secondary to 111 the sheer wonder of the setting, the atmosphere of nature at its unspoiled best. Small aircraft fly from Maun to safari camps on islands in the delta—the flight alone is a thrilling introduction to the beauty and mystery of it all. The way to explore the delta at a leisurely pace is aboard a *mokoro* (plural *mekoro*), a flat-bottomed dugout canoe poled by a knowledgeable navigator.

Moremi Wildlife Reserve

On the northeast of the Okavango Delta, the Moremi Wildlife Reserve packs a full range of landscapes into 1,800 sq km (700 sq miles)—acacia forests, floodlands, lagoons and reedy swamps. Thanks to the remarkable diversity of wilderness, the reserve can be seen by land or water or both. As varied as the terrain is the game, from lion and leopard to elephant and buffalo. And the birds—storks, herons, eagles and bee-eaters—lift the eyes and the hearts of even the least informed ornithologists.

In 1963, in an act of unprecedented generosity, local Tswana tribesmen gave this land to the nation to make sure the region's wildlife and ecosystem would never be disturbed.

DUGOUT IN THE DELTA

The local equivalent of a Venetian gondolier is the poler who propels his dugout canoe through the labyrinth of the Okavango Delta. Maps are of little use in a constantly shifting pattern of waterways, so the poler has to know where he's going—and many channels are barely deep enough for the shallow-draught boat to get through. The *mokoro*, fashioned from a single log, can accommodate three passengers. The best polers can add a lot to the experience by pointing out and identifying the birds and animals along the way.

Tsodilo Hills

Northwest of the delta, near Namibia's Caprivi Strip, four big rocky hills rise above the dunes. Thanks to the mystique of the hills and the availability of spring water, the area has been inhabited for thousands of years, as witness a profusion of rock paintings—images of animals (some now extinct), of abstractions, geometric doodles and, less frequently, of humans. They are thought to have been painted between AD 1000 and 1800 by the ancestors of the Basarwa and Bantu peoples who still inhabit the area.

Four quartzite hills stand in a row. Three of them were given names by the Bushmen: Male, Female and Child, while the smallest hill remains nameless. Most of the art work, Botswana's greatest archaeological treasure, is concentrated about the Female hill. The explorer and author Laurens van der Post called this "a Louvre of the desert". Signs of the times: vandals have desecrated some of the rock paintings with modern graffiti.

Chobe National Park

The best time to visit Chobe, in northeastern Botswana, is from May to September, when a single day's tour can reveal thousands of animals—elephants in unparalleled numbers (too many for the good of the environment), buffalo, hippo, giraffe, kudu and impala. More than 250 species of birds are also viewable. The area of the park, more than 11,000 sq km (4,500 sq miles) is about the size of Jamaica or the state of Connecticut. The accommodation ranges from crowded campsites to the sumptuous game lodge, within the park, where Richard Burton and Elizabeth Taylor spent their second honeymoon in the requisite degree of luxury.

The northern district of the park, **Serondella**, borders the Chobe River, which has its source in Angola. It provides drinking and bathing facilities for throngs of elephants and buffalo. The scenery here is an incomparable combination of flood plains and riverine woodland. Set out along the river bank, the town that services this part of the park, **Kasane**, is equipped with everything from car hire firms and safari organizers to a bank and post office.

THE BIG FIVE

There are so many elephants in Botswana's national parks, and they are such immense targets, that you can hardly miss seeing or photographing a troop. Picturesque zebra, giraffe and antelope are also abundant, but the other species of "the big five" may prove more elusive. Cape buffalo, with their great curving horns, are endangered by trophy hunters and local meat-eaters, but they should be easily visible. The leopard keeps to itself, sleeping most of the day up in a tree and hunting by night. Lions are gregarious but hard to spot in the bush; best seen around water sources in the dry season. Finally, the rhinoceros, a vegetarian, has been hunted mercilessly and makes few appearances except early morning and late afternoon at water holes.

113

A splendid stand of baobabs watching over the wasteland.

The central area of the park, **Ngwezumba**, is rich in animal life, especially when the rains have refilled the pans in, say, November to May.

The southwestern portion of the park, Savuti, is also full of fauna from November to May. The **Mababe Depression** here is the bed of an ancient lake that once covered most of northern Botswana. It is now a flat plain that comes to life when it rains. A sand ridge more than 100 km (60 miles) long shows one boundary of the great lake, which has long since dried up. Even when water is relatively scarce the animals enjoy munching the greenery.

Nxai Pan National Park

When it rains hereabouts, from November to March, the ancient lake bed turns green. Then graceful zebras, gemsboks and springboks and clumsy wildebeest flock to the Nxai Pan to nibble the grass, drink and breed. The area is also renowned for its population of giraffes and leopards. Migratory birds make this a seasonal halt, to the delight of binocular-wielding bird-watchers. A landmark south of the reserve is a grove of baobab trees, named Baines' Baobabs after Thomas Baines, the artist who painted them in 1862. Thick-trunked baobabs, known in some circles as monkey-bread trees, produce fruit which has medicinal uses. The branches also provide welcome shade, and this particular crop, forming "one magnificent shade", as Baines wrote, is really memorable.

Makgadikgadi Pans

Once upon a time there was a lake bigger than Lake Victoria here, but it all dried up—a very distant memory that's revived in the rainy season. All that's left of the prehistoric lake are large depressions called salt pans, just the sort of environment to attract waterfowl. This is the place to admire a huge blush of pink flamingoes. The plains to the west, which are not saturated with salt like the remains of the lake, abound in wildlife, especially after the rains arrive in September or October. The area is a main migration route for antelope and the predators that follow them.

For tourists, four-wheel drive is the only feasible means of locomotion for Nxai Pan and Makgadikgadi reserves.

Central Kalahari Game Reserve

In the very centre of Botswana, the world's second largest game reserve is bigger than some respectably sized European countries—for instance Denmark, Switzerland or the Netherlands. This is essentially virgin territory—no roads, no campsites—and the government has wanted to keep it that way. You need a special permit to visit the reserve.

One of the few landmarks has the strikingly evocative name of Deception Valley. Depending on the rainfall the animals may be thinner on the ground than you'd expect to find in reserves with reliable water sources. But the antelope know how to survive drought on the moisture in the vegetation. Meanwhile, the grandeur and silence of the Kalahari Desert are all around.

Kutse Game Reserve

About 240 km (150 miles) northwest of Gaborone, Kutse is the closest nature reserve to the capital, though four-wheel drive is required to get there. Elementary campsites for travellers self-sufficient in everything from water to fuel and food are the only luxury in this small reserve adjoining the Central Kalahari Game Reserve to the north.

You may encounter Bushmen who can provide knowledgeable insight into desert life and wildlife and the way to survive the Kalahari's rigours. After the rains have fallen this reserve is a gathering place for lions, leopards and their prey, and a fine range of birds.

Kgalagadi Transfrontier Park

Wildlife without frontiers: the antelope have never needed passports or visas to migrate from the Botswana portion of the national park to the South African section; in fact, there are no fences. Until 2000 the Gemsbok National Park in Botswana and the Kalahari Gemsbok National Park in South Africa were managed separately, but they have now merged and were renamed.

In the desert the game may have to travel great distances to find the water and food they require. But two usually dry rivers, the Auob and the Nossob, cut through the dunes, and when it rains they flourish. Among the animals you may see are gemsbok (whence the park's former name), wildebeest, eland and springbok—all closely followed by the lions and cheetahs who live in hope of ambushing them, and nature's competent clean-up squad of hyenas and jackals. More than 200 species of bird brighten the park. One extraordinary species, the sociable weaver bird (*Philetiarus socius*), builds gigantic nests in trees, subdivided into "apartments" for as many as 100 couples.

For most visitors the magic of the desert is the timelessness, the solitude and the rusty red sand dunes that suddenly cede to grass and trees.

ANTELOPE

They come in many varieties—elegant, stately or just plain shy. A few of the species of antelope you may spot in Botswana:

The adaptable duiker, as small as it is common, can survive on very little water.

The biggest antelope, the spiral-horned eland, looks like a cross between a cow and a deer.

The big-shouldered gemsbok has long, upright horns above a black-and-white face.

High-jump champion, the impala is reddish brown but white on the underside.

The light brown lechwe (the males have elegant swept-back horns) hang out in large, justly nervous herds close to water sources.

The handsome, horned springbok, brown with white below, move gracefully in big herds.

Mabuasehube Game Reserve

This small game reserve, on the eastern edge of the Kgalagadi Transfrontier Park, is difficult to reach, hence little visited. The name means "red soil", a curt description of the Kalahari sands,

Ivory palms in the sunset. They produce corossos, or ivory nuts, used by craftsmen as an ecological alternative to elephant ivory.

which are permeated by iron oxide. The salt pans in the Mabuasehube are a big attraction in themselves, reflecting different colours according to the time of day. During the rainy season the pans, bordered by high dunes, call together thirsty gembsbok, springbok, eland and wildebeest, followed by lions and leopards, and birds galore.

Dining Out

With two head of cattle for every inhabitant, Botswana produces a mountain of beef—a significant export commodity, with enough left over for domestic consumption. It's highly regarded for taste, though perhaps less tender than, say, the American or Argentine competition. Beef turns up on just about every restaurant menu, in the shape of steaks or burgers or meat pies. For a change, look for fried chicken or pizza. You may also be offered some of Botswana's fine river fish—bream. If you're craving fresh vegetables—and you probably will after a few days of corned beef in the bush—hasten to the buffet at one of the main hotels, where salads get pride of place.

The cuisine in general is reminiscent of British colonial days, but there are inspired exceptions 117 at some of the luxury game lodges. To outdo the competition they have hired skilled cooks who transform the best local and imported produce into inventive meals for sophisticated clients.

The diet of the average villager, by contrast, could hardly be less sophisticated. The staple is a tasteless but filling cornmeal mush called mielie-pap. Rounding out the menu are pumpkins, melons, cucumbers, beans and—for a special treat—grilled insects.

If you're in the bush you'll appreciate biltong, wind-dried strips of meat that need no refrigeration. Of beef or game, it can be as tasty as it is chewy.

Drinks

Wines from neighbouring South Africa, highly acclaimed by

DRIVING IN THE BUSH

If you're on a drive-yourself safari through Botswana's bush or desert or swamplands, you're in for a rugged experience.

The first essential is knowing your vehicle. Get used to the four-wheel-drive capability before you ever leave the comfort of the surfaced roads; have a test drive when you first encounter difficult conditions. Driving in endless tracts of sand or mud will test all your talents—and those of the vehicle.

Be on the lookout for wild animals—not just for the thrill of seeing and photographing them but to keep clear of them. Yield the right of way to any sort of livestock, from a lost goat to a troop of elephants. If animals are near, don't get out of your car or even put your arms out the windows. There are no animals, however appealing, that don't pose a danger. Don't feed any wild animal.

Driving at night, even on tarred roads, is extremely hazardous. Anything may suddenly cross your path, from ranch cattle to wild animals. The danger is heightened in winter when the paving, which retains some of the day's heat, attracts the wildlife. Use bright headlights and spotlight if available. Better yet, don't drive at all once the sun has gone down.

Although the main highways are surfaced, much of Botswana's road network consists of gravel or sand tracks. This means that oncoming traffic kicks up a great storm, cutting visibility and posing many dangers ahead. When you see someone approaching, drive very slowly or pull over and switch on your lights.

A regiment of yellow-billed hornbills complete with perch.

international experts, are widely available in Botswana. The local beer, served ice cold, is good. And a variety of familiar soft drinks rounds out the beverage repertory.

Shopping

In shopping malls, in crafts shops attached to hotels and lodges, and along the roadside the range of souvenirs for sale is dominated by basketwork. Look for baskets, trays and toys, some of a very high standard, woven from palm leaves.

Agile craftsmen also produce wood carvings, mainly inspired by the local fauna, pottery (much more interesting than mere pots) and jewellery. Weavers offer wall-hangings, tablecloths and clothing.

The Bushmen are hard to find but they create appealing beaded bracelets and belts, using tiny chips of ostrich eggshells as beads. Another unique souvenir is a Bushman bow-and-arrow hunting set.

You may be tempted by animal skins (none more striking than zebra), which are acquired from culling drives. Another aspect of the skin trade: you'll come across products of crocodile skin, such as wallets and briefcases.

119

Practical Information

Banks. Open Monday, Tuesday, Thursday and Friday 9 a.m.–2.30 p.m.; Wednesdays 8.15 a.m.–noon and Saturdays 8.15–10.45 a.m.

Climate. The seasons south of the equator are reversed. Summer, which lasts from October to April, is also the rainy season. May to September is cooler and drier. Early morning temperatures may approach the freezing point in winter.

Credit cards of most of the international brands are accepted on a limited basis. Travellers cheques may be exchanged at banks and hotels.

Customs allowance. Visitors may import duty-free 400 cigarettes and 50 cigars and 250 g tobacco; 2 litres of wine and 1 litre of alcoholic beverages; 250 ml of toilet water and 50 ml of perfume; other gift articles up to a value of P500. No restrictions on the import of foreign currency (which must be declared on arrival), but no more than P50 in local currency may be exported.

Currency. The currency of Botswana is the *Pula* (P), divided into 100 *thebe*. Banknotes come in denominations from P5 to P100, coins from 5 thebe to P5.

Driving. Roads link the main towns. Drive on the left. The speed limit on country roads is 120 km per hour (75 mph).

Electricity. 220/240 volts, 50 cycles AC.

Health. Visitors to the northern parts of the country from November to June are advised to take anti-malaria precautions.

Languages. The official languages are Setswana and English.

Photography. Ask permission before you snap local people. Don't film defence establishments, airports or official government residences.

Shops are generally open Monday to Friday 8.30 a.m.–1 p.m. and 2–5 p.m. and again on Saturday mornings.

Taxis. Fares should be agreed on before starting out.

Time. GMT + 2 all year round.

Telephone. To make an international call, dial 00 then the country code (1 for Canada and US, 44 for UK), the area code and local number. There are very few public phone boxes.

Tipping. The standard tip in urban areas is 10 per cent.

Water. Drinking water is considered safe in towns and hotels. Don't drink from (or swim in!) rivers.

ZIMBABWE

Proudly Independent

The country extends from the Limpopo in the south to the Zambezi in the north, rivers with names that evoke the heart of Africa, its mystery, rhythms and wildlife.

Lions, elephants and rhinos live here. So do 11 million people forming a mosaic of races in an independent state, with 1 million in the capital, Harare. With an area greater than 390,000 sq km (more than 150,000 sq miles)—nearly the size of California—Zimbabwe is as rich in natural resources as in natural beauty. Although the latitude is tropical, the altitude of the high plateaux makes the climate more temperate than you expect. The rainy season runs from November to March.

Shrewd old Cecil Rhodes, the English *conquistador*, knew a winner when he spotted it and foresaw a great future for this country. During his dynamic lifetime the British named the land Rhodesia, which was rather good for his ego.

But history is on the side of the pre- and post-colonial name, Zimbabwe, traceable back to the Middle Ages.

An advanced city-state built the impressive hilltop fortress of Great Zimbabwe, Africa's second largest stone structure (after the Egyptian pyramids). It flourished between the 13th and 15th centuries. The first European explorers—the Portuguese—arrived in the 16th century, checking out rumours suggesting that Zimbabwe was a new El Dorado. The reports were exaggerated. As the gold-hunting adventurers withdrew, Portuguese missionaries fanned out in search of souls to save.

Zimbabwe resisted European colonization until the end of the 19th century when the Rhodes mining group, the British South Africa Company, took over. It was a company-run country until 1923 when the British colony of Southern Rhodesia was created.

The winds of change wafted through Africa in the 1960s, but Rhodesia's white rulers were ready to risk everything to keep the status quo. They declared independence unilaterally, igniting a costly civil war with black fighters demanding majority rule. The United Nations imposed sanctions, which, at least, proved the isolated country's self-reliance. Peace returned and, in 1980, independence under majority rule. The only problems left were infighting among the black political parties, unemployment, inflation, corruption and drought, culminating in a state of turmoil ever since early 2000 when violence broke out. Touristic areas, however, remained unaffected.

A Brief History

8th–12th centuries	The ancestors of today's Shona speakers inhabit the territory of present-day Zimbabwe; they trade with coastal Arabs, exchanging rhino horns and ivory for coins, beads and Chinese porcelain.
13th–15th centuries	From the enormous dry-stone fortress of Great Zimbabwe the Shona empire rules, with elaborate court rituals and bushmen as slaves. Around 1450 the expansionist ruler Mambo Mutota presides over territory extending into today's Mozambique. But by the end of the century the kingdom is split.
16th–17th centuries	Portuguese explorers arrive, hunting the source of Zimbabwean gold. Battles with European fortune hunters weaken the empire. Portuguese colonists and missionaries accumulate power during the 17th century but are finally rebuffed by military means.
18th–19th centuries	Raids by the Zulu warrior Shaka bring turmoil to southern Africa. One of Shaka's generals, Mzilikazi, and his Ndebele followers move into the area of Zimbabwe, subjecting the Shona to vassal status. British missionaries and explorers operate in Zimbabwe. David Livingstone of the London Missionary Society discovers the Zambezi river. In 1888 King Lobengula signs a treaty of perpetual friendship with Britain. The king also signs a deal with the diamond tycoon, Cecil Rhodes, conceding him all mineral rights. In 1890, under the orders of Rhodes, white colonists from South Africa arrive in the future Rhodesia, building Fort Salisbury as their headquarters. The pioneers expropriate the land and rule by force. Lobengula fights back but in vain. In 1895 the territory changes its name officially to Southern Rhodesia.
20th century	Ruled by its white minority, Southern Rhodesia becomes a British colony. Restrictions deprive blacks of the possibility of owning desirable land, of education, health care and political power. In the 1960s Britain pressures Salisbury to give rights to the segregated black majority. Whites led by prime minister Ian Smith unilaterally declare

independence. United Nations imposes diplomatic and economic sanctions but the Rhodesian economy survives and expands. Thousands are killed in guerilla warfare. In 1980, Zimbabwe, under a black majority government, gains independence. In early 2000, members of President Mugabe's Zanu PF party occupy white farms and violence breaks out.

Sightseeing

The drama of Victoria Falls, the historic ruins of Great Zimbabwe, and no less than ten national parks: Zimbabwe has enough variety to fill several holidays. Before covering the natural highlights, we begin among all the conveniences of civilization in the national capital.

Harare

The old colonial name was Salisbury, and its founders would be surprised to see what has become of their fort today—a colourful little metropolis with parks and gardens, wide boulevards, and modern and colonial architecture. Harare, the name adopted after independence, refers to an ancient chief famous for never sleeping, or at least for being constantly alert.

The town, though, is more on the relaxed side, even if government, commerce and industry converge here. The locals take their leisure seriously in "Sunshine City", exploiting an array of recreational facilities including the area's 14 golf courses.

A couple of museums to get you started. The **National Art Gallery**, in the centre of town, displays modern art by European and Zimbabwean artists as well as traditional masks and carvings. **Queen Victoria Museum**, part of the Civic Centre complex, offers an informative preview of Zimbabwean wildlife.

Out of town, an unusual attraction is the **Tobacco Auction Rooms**. Zimbabwe is a leading producer, so the stakes are high when the growers and buyers meet—mornings from approximately April to September. The drama is open to the public.

Shona culture is highlighted at **Chapungu Kraal**, a village of thatched huts with a big display of tribal sculpture. There are music and dance performances and even a resident witch doctor. **Ewanrigg Botanical Gardens**, 40 km (24 miles) northeast of Harare, has beautiful landscaped gardens as well as unspoiled bush for a taste of the real Africa. Informative signs identify the many species of trees, plants and cactus.

THANKS, CECIL

The ruthless diamond and gold tycoon, Cecil Rhodes (1853–1902), didn't squander his wealth on high living. In his will he left some £3 million to set up the Rhodes Scholarship at Oxford University for students from the US and Commonwealth countries. (Rhodes obtained his Oxford degree rather late in life, after he'd become rich.) After their years at Oxford many of Rhodes' beneficiaries have gone on to become celebrated figures in the intellectual and political world.

Bird-spotters won't want to miss **Larvon Bird Gardens**, inhabited by more than 400 species. Farther out the Bulawayo Road, **Lion and Cheetah Park** has more lions on show than you're ever likely to spot in the game parks or anywhere else, plus cheetah, baboons and crocs.

Lake McIlwaine, the city's reservoir, is Harare's prime recreational area, busy with boating and fishing—for tiger-fish, bream and barbel. The facilities include a small game reserve where you can see antelope, zebra and giraffe. It also attracts great flocks of itinerant birds. Park service guides take visitors to see ancient rock paintings.

Bulawayo

Zimbabwe's second city, Bulawayo, was the capital of the powerful Ndebele king Lobengula. Today it's an easygoing little metropolis of more than half a million people. This close to the Kalahari desert, you might expect an arid appearance, but there's water enough to keep the city's beautiful parks and gardens lush and flourishing.

A tall white clock tower marks the **City Hall**, in the very centre of town, with the tourist information office downstairs. There's also an art gallery, the local portion of the national archives, and, outside, a market dealing in handicrafts and flowers.

On the edge of the central district, two adjoining parks—**Centenary Park** and **Central Park**—are endowed with everything from lovely flower gardens and a game reserve to a miniature railway and an olympic swimming pool. The most serious asset of Centenary Park is the modern **Museum of Natural History**, a good place for a briefing on the country's wildlife. The museum has a hoard of some 75,000 mammal specimens—said to be the largest collection in southern Africa. You can also see replicas of prehistoric cave paintings plus exhibits on history and minerals, not least gold. Outside stand old mining machines.

Nostalgia engulfs Bulawayo's **Railway Museum**. Some grand old steam locomotives have ended up here, along with a perfectly restored passenger carriage dated 1904, a museum on wheels. Bulawayo is the headquarters of the national railway system.

Matobo National Park

Weird rock formations, prehistoric bushman cave paintings, a game park and varied recreational facilities make Matobo National Park one of Zimbabwe's top tourist attractions—and it's only about 30 km (20 miles) south of Bulawayo. The terrain is so evocative that Cecil Rhodes asked to be buried here; you can see his simple tomb on the hill he called View of the World.

The **rock formations**, the result of thousands of millions of years of erosion, alternate with refreshing green valleys. The rocks were first called Matobo, meaning "bald-headed ones", by Mzilikaze, the Ndebele king. European settlers corrupted the name to Matopos, but the original has now been restored.

The Matobo game reserve is stocked with giraffe, rhino, zebra and wildebeest, and you'll also see plenty of baboons and vervet monkeys. Bird-watchers can observe what's called the world's largest concentration of black eagles.

Khami Ruins

The area of the Khami Ruins, about 20 km (12 miles) west of Bulawayo, has been inhabited for more than 100,000 years. But the ruins, the second largest complex of ancient stone structures in Zimbabwe, date from the 15th to 17th centuries. Like the Great Zimbabwe Ruins, to the east, Khami is a trove of ingenious dry-stone construction. Zulu warriors are thought to have wiped out the remaining inhabitants early in the 19th century. A small

DR LIVINGSTONE'S FOOTPRINTS

The Scottish missionary-explorer David Livingstone was the first European to see Victoria Falls—in 1855. He is well remembered: a Livingstone Memorial Statue stands beside Devil's Cataract, facing Livingstone Island. Seeing the falls moved him to write, "On sights as beautiful as this, angels in their flight must have gazed." Sixteen years later the explorer went missing. He was discovered, feverishly ill, on the shores of Lake Tanganyika by the American journalist Henry M. Stanley, who offered his hand and the memorable quote, "Dr Livingstone, I presume?"

127

museum at the site displays some of the artefacts found here, indicating that Khami's rulers traded with early European explorers and missionaries.

Hwange National Park

In the northwest corner of Zimbabwe, the country's biggest game reserve is the home of more than 100 animal species and four times as many types of birds. The star attraction is the elephant—huge herds are spotted wherever there's a waterhole. (The elephants are so abundant that they have to be culled to reduce the impact on the land and the other animals.) Also very visible are the giraffe, zebra, buffalo, and swarms of antelope of all kinds. You may have to look harder for the lion, rhino and hippo. Birdwatchers grab their binoculars and wax enthusiastic about the yellow-billed kite and the saddle-billed stork.

Hwange (formerly Wankie) National Park extends over 14,650 sq km (5,600 sq miles)—that's half the size of Belgium. Three camps are linked by nearly 500 miles (300 miles) of roads with discoveries at every turning. The park offers a variety of accommodation. There are many ways to go about seeing the wildlife, from escorted overnight hikes to moonlight safaris in minibuses to spending the night in a tree-hut overlooking a waterhole. The best season for wildlife-spotting is September and October, the dry season, when the waterholes are most crowded with animals gathered for a drink, a bath or a browse.

Victoria Falls

There is no substitute for the thrill of seeing, hearing and being showered by Victoria Falls, but some statistics set the scene. Here the Zambezi River pours 545 million litres (120 million gallons) of water per minute into a narrow chasm more than 100 m (330 ft) deep. The mist and spray may reach 500 m (more than 1,500 ft) into the sky, hence the indigenous name for the falls: Mosi-oa-Tunya, the Smoke that Thunders. The spray can be seen up to 30 km (20 miles) away. The rainbow possibilities of the world's largest waterfall are tremendous, and the surrounding terrain is so drenched that it's known as the Rain Forest.

Victoria Falls consists of five separate falls. At the western end, **Devils Cataract** is narrow but powerful. Beyond Cataract Island the **Main Falls** begin. Next come the narrow **Horseshoe Falls,** 129

Aerial view of Victoria Falls. If you come much closer, you're almost bound to get wet.

Rainbow Falls (the tallest), and the **Eastern Cataract**.

You will have to share the romance of this natural wonder with many other tourists, for Victoria Falls is one of the world's great attractions.

On the plus side, the village here—which is within walking distance of the falls—has good hotels, shops, even a casino, and agencies that organize all sorts of outings, from sensational white-water rafting to aerial excursions above the thunder.

The **Falls Craft Village**, in the centre of town, is laid out like a tribal village, but the huts have been transplanted from various regions. Artisans here demonstrate their skill at carving, basketry and other crafts. Of course their products are sold on the spot. You can also have your future told by a *nganga*.

The road from the village to the Livingstone statue goes past the **Big Tree**, a bizarre baobab of immense proportions—well over 20 m (65 ft) tall with a circumference nearly the same. They say it's more than a thousand years old.

Along the river a few kilometres north of the town, Spencer's Creek **crocodile farm** provides a wildlife experience you may not have anticipated. Several thou-

---

HAZARDS OF THE BUSH

When you think of the wildlife of the Zimbabwe bush you picture monkeys, zebras and giraffes. But it's not all charm out there. Danger can come from unexpected sources, even the tiniest insects. Here are a few to avoid.

Bilharzia, a parasite too small to see, can invade the body during a refreshing dip in a lake or river. It's a very serious matter, so stay ashore and don't drink the water.

Mosquitoes not only annoy, they can also transmit malaria, so keep covered and use repellent. You should start taking anti-malaria drugs before you leave home.

Spiders—the big, hairy type—can be as bad as they look. But the ordinary house spider is inoffensive.

Snakes come in scores of varieties. They usually want to avoid you just as strongly as you want to avoid them. If you encounter one of the nastier types—cobras, puff adders, vipers or mambas—a bite requires emergency medical help.

sand crocs of all ages and sizes are on show, and there are explanations of their breeding and living habits.

Lake Kariba

For a country without an ocean, Zimbabwe makes do with a lake covering an estimated 7,700 sq km (nearly 3,000 sq miles). Actually, it shares the body of water with another landlocked country, Zambia; the international frontier runs more or less down the middle of the long, thin lake. Lake Kariba is called Zimbabwe's tourist paradise, or the Zimbabwean Riviera. It's where the Zimbabweans go for recreation: swimming, sailing, fishing, game watching—even a flutter in a casino.

Lake Kariba, the world's fifth largest reservoir, is a man-made phenomenon, the offspring of the mighty **Kariba Dam**, a herculean hydroelectric project of the 1950s. Ten thousand men worked on construction of the dam; 87 of them died in accidents on the site. (Four who plunged into wet concrete are immured in the dam wall.)

Seeing the dam is one of the most impressive sights of a visit to Kariba. You can walk across the top of the dam—126 m (400 ft) high—to the Zambian border. At Kariba Heights, above the resort zone, **St Barbara's Chapel** was built by Italian construction workers. Designed in the shape of a coffer dam, it commemorates the men who died working on the project.

Across the lake from Kariba, the **Matusadona National Park** is the place for game watching. Look for elephant, buffalo, zebra, and birds as dramatic as openbill storks and Goliath heron.

Mana Pools

Some spectacular game viewing compensates for the remoteness

OPERATION NOAH

When they dammed the Zambezi to create Lake Kariba, the waters rose too fast for many of the indigenous animals. Many were trapped on islands that got ever smaller, then disappeared beneath the lake. The drownings touched off a wave of sympathy around the world and the government mounted a heroic rescue effort, Operation Noah, led by the conservationist Rupert Fothergill. Using boats of all types, Africa's biggest ever wildlife rescue operation saved some 5,000 animals, including 44 black rhino. A monument commemorating Operation Noah and its tireless rangers stands at Kariba Heights.

of the **Mana Pools National Park** in the Middle Zambezi Valley. The pools of the name are the bodies of water left behind when the Zambezi moved away over its convoluted geological history. For the wildlife, these ponds and brooks mean survival in the dry season (September and October) and they assemble in great numbers to show their appreciation. Elephants are plentiful, as are buffalo, antelope, zebra and hippo. The black rhinoceros, the victim of poachers in many other parts of Africa, is holding its own here. Bird-watchers will get an eyeful of Goliath heron, Egyptian geese, cormorants and storks.

Great Zimbabwe Ruins

Archaeology buffs should spare no effort to visit the Great Zimbabwe Ruins, near the town of Masvingo (formerly Nyanda/Fort Victoria). Great Zimbabwe was an African city-state that thrived in the Middle Ages, then withered late in the 15th century. In its heyday the city had a population of 10,000.

In the Shona language "zimbabwe" means "house of stone". Great Zimbabwe was built here because the climate was perfect for agriculture and the nearby hills supplied the right sort of rocks for the construction work. Literally millions of trimmed granite rocks were used to form the complex. Since mortar was unknown, gravity held up the dry-stone walls.

There are three main groups of structures. The **Hill Complex**, including the ruler's palace, later the religious centre of the community, bestrides a cliff. Here several remarkable soapstone carvings of mythological birds were found; one of them is honoured on the national flag.

The **Great Enclosure** is Africa's largest stone structure south of the Egyptian pyramids. The outer wall, with a circumference of 255 m (more than 800 ft), rises as high as 11 m (36 ft). Within are enclosures that may have had ceremonial significance, and a royal residence. The most photographed element of the Great Enclosure is the solid **Conical Tower**, 10 m (33 ft) tall, tapering from a diameter of nearly 6 m at the base to 2 m at the summit. Its purpose, other than symbolic, is not known.

The **Valley Complex**, nearby, seems to have been a residential area; some of the walls and terraces are of advanced technique. A lot of archaeological discoveries were concentrated here. You can see many of them in the Great Zimbabwe **museum**, where indigenous artefacts share the spotlight with the exotic Chinese and Arab items supplied to the Zimbabweans by foreign traders.

The Great Zimbabwe Ruins comprise the continent's greatest stone structures after the Pyramids.

Lake Kyle

If you've seen the crocodile farm, now you can discover Africa's largest lizards—in the wild. Water monitors thrive in and around Lake Kyle, just east of Great Zimbabwe. They can grow to crocodile size—more than 2 m (well over 6 ft) in length. Not the sort of reptile to cuddle up to, but fascinating to watch.

Lake Kyle, with an area of 90 sq km (35 sq miles), is popular for boating and fishing. Like the lake, the game park on the north shore is man-made: animals were introduced from other regions. One unusual feature of Muti-rikwe (Kyle) Game Park is the opportunity to view the wildlife from horseback.

Eastern Highlands

If it's too warm for you in the *highveld* terrain that characterizes most of the country, head for the Eastern Highlands and some mountain air. Splendid waterfalls, pine forests and Zimbabwe's highest mountain, **Inyangani**, rising to 2,592 m (8,500 ft), contribute to the feeling of refreshment. The mountain is climbable if you have the energy and a few hours to spare—there's a path to the summit.

The capital of the Eastern Highlands is **Mutare** (formerly 133

Umtali), a provincial town of less than 100,000 population, known as the gateway to Mozambique. Surrounded by mountains, the old-fashioned town has broad streets lined with flowering trees, and facilities that include a theatre and a concert hall in the civic centre. The local **museum** deals with the area's prehistory and history; children, among others, are fascinated by a display of authentic old steam locomotives and horse-drawn carriages; and there are snakes and birds on show. Mutare's main park includes an **aloe garden** with more than 200 species from all over Africa.

Dining Out

After roughing it in the bush, you may be ready for some pampering in the towns and resorts. The hotels lay on sumptuous buffets at affordable prices. Vegetarians and others will be impressed by the bountiful and inexpensive do-it-yourself salad bars.

Zimbabwean beef is very good. When you tire of the steaks, you can switch to game—everything is available from antelope to crocodile's tail. And for a change of culture, there are restaurants with foreign cuisines, from Italian and Greek to Indian and Chinese.

For the local folk who stick to traditional African fare, the basic food is *sadza*, a porridge of sweetcorn, usually enhanced by a meat gravy. Slightly upmarket, the *sadza* may be accompanied by bits of beef or mutton or game.

Drinks

Cold beer—lager—goes well in the African climate. Wine-lovers can experiment with Zimbabwean wine. It has been produced since 1965 and the quality is getting better all the time, even winning international awards. Try Mukuyu Winery's Pinotage/Merlot (red) and Sauvignon blanc (white), or Stapleford's Cordon Rouge (red) and their white Blanc fumé or Muscat. (These are the country's only wine producers.)

Iced non-alcoholic drinks like lemonade and ginger beer are refreshing.

Shopping

For long-lasting memories of Zimbabwe, consider the carvings, from the mass-produced to the highly artistic. Everywhere that tourists congregate, street salesmen offer attractive models of animals, carved in wood or soapstone. (Don't buy soft-wood sculptures, which are vulnerable to infiltration by insects.) On a more artistic plane, Shona artists have taken to working with hard stone, producing unusual, smooth figurines.

Beautiful traditional dance masks may be too big for your

aggage, but miniature versions re available.

For the most portable of sou-enirs, pocket some precious or emi-precious stones. They're heap and pretty, but you'd have to be an expert to know what you're really getting.

Needlework reaches some sort of zenith around Kariba, with crocheted tablecloths going for a song at roadside stalls.

Practical Information

Banks. Open Monday, Tuesday, Thursday and Friday 8 a.m.–3 p.m.; Wednesdays 8 a.m.–1 p.m. and Saturdays 8 a.m–11.30 a.m.

Climate. The seasons south of the equator are reversed. The best time to visit is April to May and August to September. The hottest month is October. The rainy season is November to March.

Credit cards of most of the international brands are widely accepted. Traveller's cheques may be exchanged at banks and hotels.

Customs allowance. Visitors may import goods up to a total of US$250 per person, including 5 litres of alcoholic beverages (for persons over 18 years), of which no more than 2 litres spirits, and also including tobacco and tobacco articles in open packages and for personal use.

Currency. The Zimbabwe dollar (Z$) is divided into 100 cents. Banknotes come in denominations from Z$2 to Z$500, coins from 1 cent to Z$5. No restrictions on the import of foreign currency (which must be declared on arrival), but no more than Z$2000 in local currency may be imported or exported.

Driving. Good roads link all the main towns. Drive on the left. The speed limit on country roads is 100 km per hour (62 mph).

Electricity. 220/240 volts, 50 cycles AC. Plugs have three square pins.

Health. Visitors to the Zambezi valley are advised to take anti-malaria precautions. From November to June the same applies to all areas below 1200 m.

Languages. The official language is English. The most widely spoken tribal languages are Shona and Ndebele.

Post offices. Open Monday to Friday 8.30 a.m.–4 p.m. and Saturday mornings until 11.30.

Shops are generally open Monday to Friday 8 a.m.–5 p.m. and again on Saturday mornings.

Taxis. In the main towns there are taxi ranks, but taxis don't cruise in search of customers.

Telephone. To make an international call, dial 110, then the country code (1 for Canada and US, 44 for UK), the area code and local number.

Time. GMT + 2.

Tipping. The standard tip is 10 to 15 per cent.

Water. Drinking water is safe in towns and hotels. Don't drink from (or swim in!) rivers or dams.

On Safari

Safari: a Swahili word meaning journey. Africa is one of the last places in the world to possess wildlife of such rich variety. The countries of Eastern and Southern Africa—especially South Africa, Botswana, Namibia, Zimbabwe, Zambia, Tanzania, Kenya and Uganda—have become world leaders in environmental protection. The size of the protected zones could cover a large part of western Europe. To get the best out of a safari, read up on all the animals before you leave home, keeping in mind, however, that you are not likely to see them all. On the one hand, some of them live in very specific habitats. On the other, changing climatic conditions and reproduction periods mean that they are visible at different times of the year. The dry season (May to October) is considered the best: that is when the animals gather round waterholes. In the south, the best time to visit the game reserves is in winter or spring (May–October). The wildebeest congregate in the southern Serengeti and calve from December to April. They start migrating northward in May, and are usually amassed in the Masai Mara from late July to October.

Mammals

Africa's mammalian fauna embraces more than 1,150 species placed in 13 orders, of which the most diverse are rodents, bats and insectivores. Of greater interest to casual safari-goers, however, is the continent's unique wealth of large mammals—from ferocious carnivores such as lion and leopard to a bewildering profusion of more placid antelopes, from the elephant and rhinoceros to man's closest living relative, the chimpanzee.

CARNIVORES

Lion *Panthera leo*

When its roar thunders over the savannah, everything stops. The lion, Africa's largest carnivore, is on the prowl. The main role of the black or golden-maned male lion is to maintain the territory of his pride, a family unit with several generations of females. Hunting is mainly a female activity, and it takes but a second for the lion's great weight and momentum to down a gazelle and break its back, or dispatch it quickly with a bite in the throat. After the kill, the male comes for his share of the meat, chasing the females away. He prefers the innards. Despite excellent teamwork, lions do not have a high success rate: four times out of five the prey gets away. Sprawled out beneath a tree, lions generally sleep 20 hours a day. Feverish activity breaks out only when the females are in heat: they can mate up to 80 times daily! It takes their mind off their food. While the females always stay together, the males are chased out after a few years by a rival group. When the dominant male is deposed, the new master of the harem will kill or expel the male cubs of previous litters.

Leopard *Panthera pardus*

The most elusive of Africa's large cats is the leopard, which generally snoozes by day, draped over a high branch hidden by the foliage. At nightfall, when it's time to start

African queen

Claude Hervé-Bazin

At home up a tree

Cheetah *Acinonyx jubatus*

The cheetah is the world's fastest mammal, capable of running at 110 kph (68 mph) to overtake the quickest antelope. A plains dweller, it bursts from the high grass to pursue its prey, but can't maintain high speeds for long and usually gives up an fruitless chase after 500 m. The most diurnal hunter of Africa's large predators, the cheetah has a success rate of 50 percent, twice as good as the lion's. Standing about 1 m (3 ft) tall at the shoulder, and weighing 40–60 kg, the cheetah is easily distinguished from the superficially similar but bulkier leopard by its greyhound build, small round head (with diagnostic black "tear marks" running from eye to mouth) and single as opposed to compound spots. It is the only large feline in the world placed outside the genus *Panthera* (big cats), due to certain anomalous features such as non-retractable claws. The female gives birth to up to five cubs, but it's rare for more than two to survive beyond 3 months, particularly where densities of rival predators are high.

hunting, the perch becomes a lookout. The leopard is quite a gourmet, ready to taste anything from insects to crocodiles, but its main prey consists of baboons or small to medium-sized antelope such as gazelles, which it hauls up to the hideout with the help of strong jaws and 70 kg of muscle. The leopard's beautiful tan coat is dotted with circular black "rosettes". In certain high-altitude areas such as the Aberdare Mountains, melanistic individuals (panthers) are regularly born into otherwise ordinary litters. Unlike the lion, the leopard is a solitary creature; the male stays with the female only during the mating season.

Record-breaker

Claude Hervé-Bazin

Bernard Joliat

Acrobatic cat

Serval *Felis serval*

This solitary medium-sized cat is about one-third as bulky as the cheetah and has a similar coat: tawny with rows of black spots along the back. You may catch sight of its pointed, white-patched ears sticking up above high grass. Found in African bush country, the serval feeds on rodents, insects and frogs. A nocturnal animal, it has a novel hunting method that consists of jumping high into the air and letting itself drop onto the unfortunate prey, knocking it out. It can even catch birds in flight.

African wild cat *Felis sylvestris*

The direct ancestor of the domestic cat, and similar in appearance to a tabby, but with longer legs, the African wild cat is found throughout eastern and southern Africa, but seldom seen as it hunts at night and hides during the day.

Caracal *Felis caracal*

The caracal is the African equivalent of the lynx: a medium-sized sandy-coloured cat with black facial mark-ings and distinctive long-tufted ears. Tolerant of a wide variety of habitats, it is most common in dry rocky savannah, but like the serval it is a secretive nocturnal hunter and seldom observed.

Tufty

African wild dog *Lycaon pictus*

Also known as the hunting or painted dog, Africa's largest canid has rounded ears, long legs, black skin and a sparse, mottled fur of black, yellow and white. Highly sociable, it lives and travels in packs of up to 50 individuals, with a majority of males. Within packs, usually only one couple does all the breeding. Of all African animals, it is the best hunter and incredibly ferocious, hunting in relays,

Spotted dog

which obstinately pursue their prey until it collapses exhausted. Persecuted in some areas and eliminated by rabies elsewhere, the wild dog is highly endangered, with an estimated 5,000 remaining in the wild. The most important stronghold is the vast Selous Game Reserve, with at least 1,000 individuals. Wild dogs are quite common in the Kruger National Park.

Jackals *Canis spp*
Placed in the same genus as domestic dogs—which they resemble in appearance and behaviourally—two species of jackal are widely distributed in eastern and

Lovesick

southern Africa. The black-backed jackal *(C. mesomelas)* is associated with acacia habitats, and is more common than the side-striped jackal *(C. adustus)* except in the miombo woodland belt of Zimbabwe, Zambia and southern Tanzania. Both species are fawn-brown with a silvery-black back, but wide regional variation in coloration means that the most reliable way to tell them apart is by the colour of the tail tip—white in the side-striped but black in the black-backed. The common (or Eurasian) jackal *(C. aureus)* is a northern species whose range extends south to central Tanzania—all three species cohabit the Serengeti-Ngorongoro ecosystem in northern Tanzania. Jackals are opportunistic omnivores, feeding on anything from carrion, freshly hunted birds and mammals, and fruits and bulbs. Their soul-searching musical howl, a love call, is a characteristic sound of the African night.

Ulrich Ackermann

Family values

Bat-eared fox *Otocyon megalotis*
Associated with dry acacia savannah, the bat-eared fox is an endearing small canid with a thick grey-red coat, large ears and a distinctive black "robber's mask" around the eyes. Generally seen in pairs, sometimes with offspring in tow, it is particularly visible in Tanzania's Serengeti and South Africa's Kalahari Gemsbok National Parks.

Hyenas
Dog-like in appearance, but more closely related to genets and civets, Africa's four hyena species are all characterized by a sloping back and limping gait. Ubiquitous in most habitats other than desert and rainforest, the spotted hyena *(Crocuta crocuta)* is Africa's second bulkiest carnivore, noted for emitting an array of whoops and giggles that resound menacingly through the night. Often portrayed as an exclusive scavenger, it actually hunts 60 per cent of its prey. In addition, thanks to a highly developed sense of smell and powerful jaws adapted for crushing bones, it does an excellent job of keeping the landscape clean. The spotted hyena lives in loose clans of 20 to 50 individuals, in which females are dominant over males. In ancient times, the spotted hyena was thought to be hermaphroditic due to the female's unique external genitalia, which consist of a penis-like clitoris and sacs resembling a scrotum.

Scarcer and more localized, the handsome striped hyena *(Hyaena hyaena)*, with its distinctive black-and-cream striped coat and long shaggy spinal crest, is a northern species whose range extends into drier parts of Kenya and Tanzania. The brown hyena *(Hyaena brunnea)*, restricted to Botswana, Namibia and bordering regions of Zimbabwe and South Africa, can be recognized by its lustrous brown coat and cream neck cape.

The aardwolf *(Proteles cristata)*, an elusive resident of semi-arid country, superficially resembles a miniature striped hyena, but feeds almost exclusively on harvester termites.

Pungent

Hunting for pleasure

Civet *Civettictis civetta*

In the 17th century, the civet was still found in Europe, where its musk—squirted out defensively into an enemy's face or to scent its territory—was used in the perfume industry as a fixative. The African civet has a long heavy torso marked with black and tan spots and stripes, and a pointed weasel-like muzzle. Seldom observed by day, it is often seen sniffing along the ground on night drives. Although predominantly carnivorous, it also feeds on fruits.

Genet *Genetta spp*

This genus of roughly 10 small nocturnal carnivore species is distinguished from the closely related civet by a more streamlined appearance, relatively lightly spotted coat and long slinky black-ringed tail. Genets also differ from civets in having retractable claws, allowing them to climb trees with ease. To hunt, the genet slinks stealthily through the grass before pouncing on its prey; it seems to kill partly for pleasure as it never finishes all of its meal. The two most common species are the small-spotted genet *(G. genetta)* and large-spotted genet *(G. tigrina)*, which can be differentiated by their tail tips—respectively cream and black. Among the most beautiful and graceful of African predators, genets are very habituated at some lodges, where they wander through the dining room oblivious to human observers.

Mongooses

The 23 species of African mongoose have in common a pup-like face with small eyes and ears, a slender body, relatively uniform coloration, and strongly terrestrial habits. Contrary to legend, no African mongoose feeds mainly on snakes—insects, rodents, lizards, carrion, crustaceans and even fruits form the core diet of various species. Most African mongooses are solitary and nocturnal, including the large white-tailed mongoose *(Ichneumia albicauda)*, which is often observed on night drives in savannah habitats. The two mongoose 143 species most likely to be seen on safari are both highly sociable and mainly diurnal. These are the banded mongoose *(Mungos mungo)*, distinguished by its faintly striped grizzled grey coat, and the dwarf mongoose *(Helogale parvula)*, often seen poking their heads inquisitively from burrow entrances in a termite mound. The most socially sophisticated mongoose is the suricate or meerkat *(Suricata suricata)*, a denizen of the arid western half of southern Africa. The main group will sit together on their haunches, while a sentry is posted on the nearest vantage point to raise the alarm when an intruder enters their territory—at which point the whole group scurries off into the safety of its subterranean burrow network.

On the alert

WWF.Klein & Hubert/BIOS

144

Sweet tooth

Honey badger *Mellivora capensis*
Also known as the ratel, this unmistakable medium-sized carnivore, jet black but with a silvery white back, is best-known for its custom of raiding beehives for honey, but it is also an adept hunter and forager. Its pugilistic build reflects a legendary pugnacious temperament. The honey badger might be seen singly or in pairs towards dusk in any savannah reserve, but sightings are rare.

PRIMATES

Common chimpanzee
Pan troglodytes
Man's closest living relative is a rainforest species whose range extends as far east as Lake Tanganyika in western Tanzania. Chimpanzees live in extended communities of up to 150 individuals, and their home territories are fiercely protected by the males, which—unlike the more mobile females—seldom leave the community into which they were born. Tan-

zania's population of 2,000 wild chimpanzees represents 1 per cent of the continental total, but it's well protected and has been the subject of extensive research, most famously by Jane Goodall in Gombe Stream. Here, and in the Mahale Mountains National Park, habituated chimps can be approached within metres on guided foot excursions.

Africa's other two great ape species, the bonobo and gorilla, are absent from southern Africa, Kenya and Tanzania, but habituated gorilla troops can be visited in Uganda.

Baboon *Papio papio*

The size of a large dog, with a long, canine face and fearsome jaw, the baboon is a gregarious animal, living in troops of up to 100 members, under the authority of a dominant male. If the ruler takes priority for food and delousing, it does not enjoy the privileges of a harem, for when the females are in heat they offer themselves to any available partner. Powerful and aggressive, baboons are common residents of savannah habitats throughout eastern and southern Africa, but are most prolific in open, rocky territory and avoid forests.

The Thinker

Claude Hervé-Bazin

Big boss

Three races—regarded by many authorities as full species—are found in the region. The olive baboon (*P. p. anubis*), which occurs in East Africa west of the Rift Valley, is the bulkiest and most imposing, weighing up to 50 kg and also with a prominent cape. The paler and more lightly built yellow baboon (*P. p. cynocephalus*) ranges east of the Rift Valley, and is replaced by the dark grey chacma baboon (*P. p. ursinus*) in southern Africa.

Photodisc Collection

Forest guenons
Cercopithecus spp

The guenons of the genus *Cercopithecus* are mostly forest monkeys of West/Central Africa, the most notable

Vervet monkey

Sykes monkey

146 *Red-tailed monkey*

exception (aside from the savannah-dwelling vervet) being the cryptically coloured blue or Sykes monkey *(C. mitis)*, a localized resident of riverine and other forests in eastern and southern Africa. Little larger than a cat, the vervet monkey *(C. aethiops,* can be recognized by its grizzled grey coat, black face, fringe of long white hairs, and the male's bright blue scrotum. An adaptable and opportunistic omnivore, it is an unusually terrestrial monkey, and troops of 20 or more are ubiquitous except in deserts and forest interiors. Habituated vervet monkeys often live in the vicinity of lodges, making frequent raids on the buffet table.

Two other guenon species occur in Kenya or Tanzania. The red-tailed monkey *(C. ascanius)*, easily recognized by its bold white nose patch, occurs in forested habitats in southwestern Kenya and around Lake Tanganyika. De Brazza's monkey *(C. neglectus)*, distinguished by its striking white beard, is resident in Kenya's Saiwa Swamp National Park.

Patas monkey
Erythrocebus patas

Like the baboon and vervet, the patas is a terrestrial monkey, but it has a spindlier build, a reddish coat and a black stripe above the eyes. Its core range is the dry savannah of the Sahel, extending into the northwest of Kenya, but an isolated population lives in Tanzania's Serengeti National Park.

Patas monkey

Colobus monkeys

The colobus monkeys are medium-sized, thumbless forest-dwellers that subsist largely on leaves and live in troops of 10 to several hundred individuals. Absent from southern Africa, they are well represented in East Africa, in particular the spectacular black and white colobus *(Colobus guereza)*, which occurs in most montane and some lowland forests. The Central African red colobus *(Piliocolobus oustaleti)* is a Congolese species whose range extends into Gombe Stream and Mahale Mountains National Parks, where it is reg-ularly hunted by chimpanzees. Three red colobus species endemic to East Africa are listed as endangered by the IUCN, none boasting populations of greater than 2,000. Kirk's red colobus *(P. kirkii)*, notable for its unkempt white fringe, is unique to Zanzibar, and is readily approached in Jozani Forest Reserve. The Iringa red colobus *(P. gordonorum)* and Tana River red colobus *(P. rufomitratus)* are respectively confined to the Udzungwa Mountains (Tanzania) and the Tana River (Kenya).

Bushbabies

Bushbabies are primitive nocturnal primates, closely related to the lemurs of Madagascar, with soft woolly fur, large round eyes and a tail longer than the body. Several species are recognized, of which the largest is the rabbit-sized greater galago *(Otolemur crassicaudatus)*. You may see one leaping from branch to branch on a night drive, but are more likely to hear its piercing scream.

Black and white colobus

Bundle of fur

147

BOVINES

Africa's bovines are comprised of some 80 species of antelope—ranging in size from the 2-kg pygmy antelope to the 950-kg eland—as well as a solitary wild cattle species. Admired for their speed and grace, most African antelopes are strikingly handsome, and have one thing in common: they are a choice item on the menu of big cats and other large predators.

African buffalo *Syncerus caffer*
A member of the wild ox family, the burly buffalo bulldozes its way through life. All the animals of the savannah, including the normally fearless lion, are wary of it. A wounded buffalo is all the more bad-tempered, and its heavy curved horns can easily rip a victim apart. Most of the time, however, buffaloes mind their own business, grazing peacefully in herds of up to 2,000 head. The smaller, redder forest buffalo is a West African race whose range extends into parts of Uganda.

Bulldozer

Eland

Common eland *Taurotragus oryx*
With a shoulder height of up to 1.8m (6 ft), the common eland is the world's largest antelope—heavier even than the massive buffalo. It has heavy folds of skin hanging from the neck and spirally twisting horns. Despite its weight, it can gallop as fast as a horse and make quite impressive jumps. Its hair is short and fawn-coloured, with vertical white lines behind the hump on its back.

Greater kudu
Tragelaphus strepsiceros
The second-largest African antelope, the stately greater kudu, is common in southern Africa, but scarce further north, having been all but eliminated by rinderpest in the 1890s. The male

Claude Hervé-Bazin

Male kudu

Female kudu

has magnificent corkscrew horns that can reach 1 m in length. The coat is light brown, bluish grey down the sides with narrow white bands. It has a long tuft of hair hanging from the throat. It typically lives in herds of 5–10 individuals, with the sexes mingling only in the breeding season, when the males clash in thundering duels.

Lesser kudu *(T. imberbis)*

Absent from southern Africa, the lesser kudu looks similar to the greater kudu, but is smaller, darker and marked with extra stripes—including a white arrow between the eyes. Generally timid, small herds are most likely to be seem in semi-arid reserves such as Ruaha National Park (Tanzania) and Samburu National Reserve (Kenya).

Ariadne van Zandbergen

Bushbuck

Bushbuck *Tragelaphus scriptus*

Widespread and common, the bushbuck is a rather shy and solitary inhabitant of thicket and forest. It is a very handsome creature, with a dark chestnut coat, a "harness" of two horizontal white stripes on the flanks, and half a dozen vertical stripes on each side. The male has short, streamlined, spiralling horns which help it to force through the bush.

Nyala *Tragelaphus angasi*

Restricted to the eastern lowveld of southern Africa, the nyala is quite common within its limited range, par- 149

Bernard Joliat

Nyala

ticularly in northern KwaZulu Natal. The male, slate grey in colour, has a splendid fringe of brown hair on the throat and under the belly, in addition to a long white mane from shoulder to tail. The female is smaller and reddish brown, with sharply defined white stripes. Only the males have horns, which are lyre-shaped and seem particularly threatening to adversaries in the combats that take place in the rutting season.

Claude Hervé-Bazin

Sitatunga

Sitatunga *Tragelaphus spekei*
The swamp-dwelling sitatunga has very long, slender hooves and spreading toes which help it move over soft mud. In case of danger, it dives underwater and swims away. The fur is soft and brown, lighter in the female, with white stripes and dots on the sides. Although widespread, the sitatunga is often elusive due to the inaccessibility of its favoured habitat. Reliable sites include Rubondo Island (Tanzania), Saiwa Swamp (Kenya) and the Okavango Delta (Botswana).

Bongo

Bongo *Tragelaphus eurycerus*
The bongo is a large forest antelope with a rich chestnut coat, a dozen vertical white stripes on the body, a white band from eye to eye, and a short, stubby mane. It is represented in East Africa by one isolated population in Kenya's Aberdare National Park.

Reedbuck *Redunca spp*
Three species of reedbuck are recognized: bohor *(R. redunca)*, southern *(R. arundinum)* and mountain *(R.*

Reedbuck

fulvorufala). All three are slender, light brown, and stand about 75 cm (30 in) tall at the shoulder. The bohor and southern reedbuck frequent marshes and grassland near water, with the former essentially restricted to eastern Africa and the latter to southern Africa, though their ranges overlap in Tanzania. The mountain reedbuck has a prominent patch of naked skin beneath the ear—a scent gland for marking its territory.

Waterbuck *Kobus ellipsiprymnus*
The waterbuck is a powerful animal, dark brown in colour and defensive of its territory. The male sports a pair of long, ridged horns that form a graceful U-shape. It lives near lakes, waterholes and rivers and is a good swimmer, taking refuge in the water when pursued. Two distinctive races of waterbuck exist. The common waterbuck (southern Africa and East Africa east of

Waterbuck

the Rift Valley) is greyish in colour and has prominent white crescents on its rump, while the Defassa waterbuck (East Africa west of the Rift Valley) has a more rufous coat and a full white rump.

Oryx *Oryx gazella*
The oryx, according to the ancient Egyptians, could multiply at will the number of its horns, while the Greeks thought it had only one horn—which may have given rise to the legend of

Oryx

the unicorn. Equine in build and sandy grey in colour, the oryx has black markings on its face and forelegs and a triangular head with straight horns. Three geographically isolated races—regarded by some authorities as full species —live in hot dry climates, where they can survive for long periods without water. The Beisa oryx *(O. g. beisa)* has long, straight horns and is confined to northeast Kenya and Ethiopia. The fringe-eared oryx *(O. g. callotis)* has little tufts of hair on the points of its ears, and is restricted to southeast Kenya and northern Tanzania. A common resident of drier parts of southern Africa, the gemsbok *(O. g. gazella)* has rapier-like horns that curve slightly backwards and are used for fighting.

Sable antelope *Hippotragus niger*
Localized and elusive, the sable is a remarkably elegant antelope, in par-

ticular the male, with its black coat, contrasting white belly and snout, and sickle-shaped horns that grow to 1.5 m long. The sable inhabits miombo woodland in southern Tanzania, Zambia and Zimbabwe, where the largest population—as high as 30,000—is protected within the Selous Game Reserve. It is common near Pretoriuskop in the Kruger National Park, and an isolated population is easily observed in Shimba Hills National Reserve (Kenya).

Roan antelope

Roan antelope
Hippotragus equinus
Similar in appearance to the smaller but more spectacularly horned sable, the roan has a greyish-brown coat offset by a black and white face. The males are extremely aggressive and engage in bloody battles during the rutting season. Widely distributed in the miombo woodland of Zambia, Zimbabwe and Angola, the roan is elsewhere common in Tanzania's Ruaha National Park and the northern Kruger National Park.

Ariadne van Zandbergen

Sable antelope

Grant's gazelle *Gazella granti*

In proportion to its body, Grant's gazelle has the longest horns of all

Grant's gazelle

the antelopes: those of the male can measure as much as 70 cm to a shoulder height of 1 m. A graceful beast, admired for its big dark eyes, it lives in large herds in the plains and grasslands of East Africa. It can be distinguished from Thomson's gazelle by its white tail. Its hindquarters, also white, are marked by vertical black stripes.

Thomson's gazelle

Thomson's gazelle
Gazella thomsoni

Slender and elegant, Thomson's gazelle has two wide black bands diagonally crossing its flanks. The hindquarters are also white, outlined in black. The tail, perpetually in movement, is dark. During the dry season, the gazelles collect in large herds numbering thousands on the plains of East Arica.

Springbok *Antidorcas marsupialis*
South Africa's national emblem—and the only gazelle found in southern Africa—looks very similar to Thomson's gazelle, with the same coat, the same black side-band, and the same dark stripe on the sides of its face. However, its tail is white and its horns are finer. A white patch on the hindquarters contains scent glands. Capable of overtaking a moving vehicle, the springbok can jump (or

Claude Hervé-Bazin

Springbok

"pronk") more than 2 m in the air, which it does when alarmed.

Gerenuk *Litocranius walleri*

With its interminable, slender neck, the gerenuk can stretch higher than most other antelopes to reach the acacia leaves and twigs that form its diet. It often stands on its long hind legs to nibble as far up the tree as possible. It lives in arid regions and

154 *Gerenuk*

can go without water for long periods. Its fur is dark beige and its horns rather short. Absent from southern Africa, it is widely distributed in arid parts of East Africa, in particular Samburu National Reserve and Tsavo East.

Blue wildebeest

Connochaetes taurinus

With horns like handlebars and a cow's head, a skinny body, bushy

Blue wildebeest

beard and long fly-swatter tail, the wildebeest (or gnu, as the Hottentots say) resembles an African version of the bison. In summer, the mass migration of hundreds of thousands of white-bearded wildebeest, crossing the plains of East Africa in search of fresh grass, makes an impressive spectacle. It braves every danger: attacks by big cats, crocodile-infested rivers, and the birth of calves along the way. In South Africa, the local sub-species has a black beard.

Black wildebeest
Connochaetes gnou
Endemic to the grassy South African highveld and Swaziland, this formerly common antelope—darker than the blue wildebeest and with a distinctive white tail —has been reduced by hunting to an estimated 4,000 individuals, many protected on private ranches. A good place to look for it is Golden Gate National Park.

Hartebeest *Alcelaphus buselaphus*
Found in fairly large herds on the grassy savannah and plains of East Africa, where it frequently accompa-

(southern Tanzania and Zambia) is regarded by some authorities as a full species, with horns that close together like a scorpion's pincers. Those of the tawny Jackson's hartebeest are somewhere between the two, forming a U-shape. The red hartebeest of southern Africa has a paler, rustier coloration than the more northerly races.

Topi *Damaliscus lunatus*
Known as the tsessebe in southern Africa, the topi is closely related to the hartebeest and similar in overall appearance, but much darker. Com-

Hartebeest

Topi

nies zebras and wildebeest on their migration, this animal is easily identified by its stately air, its exceptionally long face, and its shiny coat. Seven races are recognized, each with a distinctive horn shape. Most common in East Africa is Coke's hartebeest, sandy in colour and with widespread lyre-shaped horns mounted on bony pedestals covered with hair. Lichtenstein's hartebeest

mon on the grassy plains of East Africa, it is usually seen in small family groups, but occasionally travels in herds of several hundred.

Blesbok *Damaliscus dorcas*
Endemic to South Africa, this lightly built relation of the topi was hunted close to extinction in the 19th century and most of the extant population is essentially domestic. Two very dis- 155

Claude Hervé-Bazin

Blesbok

tinct races occur: the blesbok *(D. d. albifrons)* of the highveld has a white blaze on the forehead and greenish-yellow horns, while the more handsome bontebok *(D. d. pygargus)* of the Cape fynbos has a white tail and "socks". A good place to see them is the Bontebok National Park near Swellendam.

Impala *Aepyceros melampus*

Another acacia-eater, the impala has a definite spring in its step: it can clear 10 m in length and 3 m in height with no problem at all. When danger threatens, the whole herd starts jumping around in apparent disorder, thoroughly confusing the predators. The male, beneath its hand-some pair of lyre-shaped horns, lords it over a harem of up to 100 females. Superficially similar to gazelles, but more closely related to wildebeest and hartebeest, the impala can be easily recognized by its long neck, triangular head and three black stripes on the tail and hindquarters; if any doubt subsists, look at the rear hooves, which are fetchingly fringed by a tuft of black hairs. Arguably the most successful antelope species, the impala is abundant in most acacia habitats in eastern and southern Africa.

Duikers

Duikers are small secretive forest antelope characterized by sloping backs and richly coloured coats. Most of the 18 recognized species are confined to West Africa, but the blue duiker *(Caphalophus monticola)* is common in the forests of the eastern coastal belt, as are the red duiker *(C. natalensis)* and Harvey's duiker *(C. harveyi)*, south and north of the Tanzania-Mozambique border respectively. The endangered Ader's duiker *(C. adersi)*, endemic to coastal woodland in East Africa, is virtually

Impala

Red duiker

Claude Hervé-Bazin

Oribi

xtinct except on Zanzibar Island. he larger Abbott's duiker *(C. padix)* is confined to a few montane orests in Tanzania. The common duiker *(Sylvicapra grimmia)*, the only avannah dwelling duiker, is locally ery common.

Other small antelope

As many as a dozen small antelope pecies occur eastern and southern Africa. One of the most distinctive is he klipspringer *(Oreotragus oreoragus)*, an agile resident of rocky ills, some 50 cm high at the shoulder, with a grizzled yellowish-brown oat, long ears, and short spiked

horns. The oribi *(Ourebia ourebi)* is about the same size as the klipspringer, but lives in tall grassland, and has a light tan coat, black tail tip, and diagnostic black scent gland behind the eye. Smaller than the above is Kirk's dikdik *(Madoqua kirkii)*, a savannah and thicket species, with small, straight horns projecting backwards, bold white eye rings, and an unusual protruding nose.

Klipspringer

Ulrich Ackermann

Dikdik

MISCELLANEOUS

Giraffe
Giraffa camelopardalis

A fully grown giraffe could look through a second-floor window without having to stretch. In the open brush, its 2-m-long neck enables it to reach the leaves of acacia trees, its principal source of food. Its hairy lips and long, prehensile tongue, 40 cm (15 in) long, act as protection against the acacia's sharp thorns. With such a limited diet, the giraffe has to spend at least 20 hours a day just eating. As it only needs 20 minutes' sleep, it passes most of the time between meals gazing at the landscape (it has excellent eyesight, a wide range of vision and long, flirty eyelashes). On the tip of its tail is a tuft of long hair that is used as a fly swatter. Its neck only has seven cervical vertebra, the same as all other mammals, but each neck bone is greatly elongated—and a strong heart is needed to pump sufficient blood all the way up to the head. To reach anything on the ground, or to drink, the giraffe has to adopt an ungainly posture, spreading its front legs wide.

Several races are recognized. The southern giraffe of southern Africa and Maasai giraffe of Tanzania and southern Kenya both have a colour pattern of dark blotches on a paler background. The striking reticulated giraffe of northern Kenya has quadrangular markings separated by sharply defined narrow white lines. The rare Rothschild's giraffe, most easily seen in Kenya's Lake Nakuru National Park, is distinguished by an extra pair of horns, and a lack of spots beneath the knee.

Fancy dress

Hippopotamus
Hippopotamus amphibius

The name literally translates from the Latin as "river horse". Most of the time, pods of a few dozen wade around close to the banks, grunting loudly, but otherwise invisible except for their nostrils and ears poking discreetly above the surface. The nostrils have flaps that close when the animal submerges. The big yawns in which hippos indulge don't mean they are tired: the male opens wide to impress its adversaries with its sharp sickle-like teeth, up to 60 cm in length. Battles between male hippos can be extremely violent and sometimes result in the death of the weaker individual. The hippopotamus normally leaves the water only at night, to graze on the riverbanks—leaving behind piles of droppings to mark its territory.

Swine

The warthog *(Phacochoerus aethiopicus)* is a widespread savannah resident named for the large warts that grow on each side of its long, flat face. It has a bristly mane, long tusks, and a rather comic habit of running off with its tail raised stiffly in the air. Largely diurnal, the warthog is often seen in small family groups, in a characteristic kneeling position, snuffling around for roots and insects.

Larger, hairier and darker, the bushpig *(Potamochoerus larvatus)* is not uncommon, but it is seldom seen due its nocturnal habits and preference for thickets and forest. The giant forest hog *(Hylochoerus meinertzhageni)*, the world's bulkiest pig—up to 250 kg—is essentially a West African species, but isolated populations persist in certain highland forests in Kenya and northern Tanzania. Both

Ulrich Ackermann

Ugly mug

forest swine are seen regularly at The Ark in Aberdare National Park and Mountain Lodge on the border of Mount Kenya National Park.

Rhinoceroses

The more widespread of Africa's two rhino species, the black rhinoceros *(Diceros bicornis)* is known for its bad temper, poor eyesight and tiny brain, a combination that sees it habitually charging towards anything that moves, including trains, and sometimes things that don't! The white rhinoceros *(Ceratotherium simum)*, though significantly bulkier (up to 1,600 kg as opposed to 1,100 kg), is far more placid. Size aside, the main physical difference between black and white rhinos is their lip shape—the upper lip of the

Claude Hervé-Bazin

River horse

black rhino forms a pointed hook to clip twigs and leaves, while the white rhino has wide square lips suitable for grazing. It is this—"white" being a mistranslation of the African "weit", meaning wide—that has led to the names white and black rhino.

Rhinoceroses are now locally extinct or headed that way in several reserves that supported populations of several thousand as recently as the 1970s. The main cause of this poaching is the Oriental belief that the horn is a strong aphrodisiac—a legend that might be linked to the animal's lengthy coition, lasting up to an hour. Today, the main stronghold of both species is South Africa, where white and black rhino are protected in significant numbers in the Kruger National Park and various Zululand reserves. The white rhino is almost extinct further north,

but isolated populations of black rhino occur in the Tanzania's Ngorongoro Crater and some private reserves in Kenya.

Zebra *Equus spp*

To human observers, the distinctive black-and-white striped coat of the zebra may seem to defeat the pur-

Optical illusions

pose, but this camouflage system does work very well in the bush. Blurred by the heat haze, the mingled silhouettes of the herd create a dazzling optical illusion that completely throws predators. It confuses the lions, and is even thought to spoil the aim of pesky insects. A gregarious animal, the zebra shares its territory with wildebeest and antelopes. It lives in herds numbering several dozen, and during the migratory season can travel in groups of a thousand or more.

Three species of zebra are recognized. The widespread plains zebra *(E. burchelli)* is a common savannah resident through-

Armoured tank

Claude Hervé-Bazin

out eastern and southern Africa, with the more southerly races characterized by light brown "shadows" between the black stripes. The endangered Grevy's zebra (*E. grevyi*), almost twice as bulky and more narrowly striped, is restricted to arid plains in northern Kenya and Ethiopia. Two races of mountain zebra (*E. zebra*) are endemic respectively to South Africa and Namibia, where they can be distinguished from local races of plains zebra by the absence of shadow stripes. The Cape mountain zebra (*E. z. zebra*) is an endangered fynbos inhabitant of the southern Cape, where fewer than 1000 surviving individuals are protected in various provincial reserves. An estimated 7,000 Hartmann's mountain zebra (*E. z. hartmannae*) survive in the arid coastal belt of Namibia.

Elephant *Loxodonta africana*

The largest animal walking the earth can weigh over 6.5 tonnes, which is perhaps not surprising when you consider that it never stops growing during all of its 80 years. The longest pair of tusks on record measured 3.49 m and weighed 200 kg, but those of an average elephant are around 1 m in length. Heavier and taller than its Asian cousin, the African elephant also has different-shaped ears and trunk. This strange nasal appendage is a magical, multi-purpose tool, extremely flexible thanks to its 500 muscles. It enables the elephant to feed, smell, feel, break off branches, fell trees, lift and carry, shoo flies, and give itself a shower! It also makes an excellent snorkel to help the animal through deep water. They say an elephant never forgets, and it does indeed have a good memory, even though the brain is rather small in proportion to the whole body.

A normal drink for an elephant is about the equivalent of a full bathtub; it downs 10 litres at a time in one gulp. It is always hungry and eats all day long, needing about a tenth of its body weight per day to keep going—300 kg of leaves, bark, roots and fruit ground up by the molars (weighing 4 kg each). These are renewed five times during the animal's lifetime, but once the last set has gone, many aged elephants die of hunger as they can no longer feed themselves.

Claude Hervé-Bazin

Africa's heavyweight

Hyraxes

Although they look like overgrown, tail-less rats, hyraxes are more closely related to elephants than to rodents. The rock hyrax *(Procavia capensis)*, a sociable vegetarian associated with rocky outcrops, is capa-

Claude Hervé-Bazin

Rat or pachyderm?

ble of ascending near-vertical rocks thanks to its friction-padded feet. The nocturnal tree hyrax *(Dendrohyrax arboreus)* almost never comes down to the ground, and emits an utterly spine-chilling shrieking cry.

Aardvark *Orycteropus afer*

Placed in a unique order, this amazing insectivore combines characteristics of many other animals: a vaguely pig-like snout and feet, long rabbit-like ears, and a body and tail something like the kangaroo. Nocturnal and solitary, the aardvark breaks open termite nests with its claws and captures the insects with its long, sticky tongue. It can fight but usually, when attacked, it will hastily dig out a burrow.

Ant-eating pig

Pangolin *Manis spp*

Shy and timorous, the pangolin, or scaly anteater, is clad in a coat of mail strong enough to withstand all attacks. When threatened, it rolls up into a tight ball like a hedgehog and lifts its scales towards the aggressor. These are so sharp they can scratch metal! A nocturnal animal, the pangolin feeds on termites and ants, catching them with its exceedingly long, sticky tongue. It is toothless, but can tear apart termite nests with its front claws. There are four kinds of pangolins in Africa, the largest of which, *M. gigantea*, can measure 1.5 m (5 ft) in length.

Armour-plated

Reptiles

Southern Africa can boast more than 400 species of reptile—cold-blooded, scaly animals—including 130 species of snake.

Snakes

Possibly the most feared of all vertebrates, snakes are abundant in Africa, but thankfully also very timid and secretive, and unlikely to be encountered unless actively searched for. Most snakes are non-venomous, and fatal bites are rare (in South Africa, lightning accounts for a greater number of deaths than snakebites!), but it is wise to wear heavy boots and long trousers when walking in the bush as a precaution. The largest African snake—up to 7m long—is the rock python *(Python sebae)* which feeds on small mammals it strangles to death.

Lizards

More conspicuous than snakes, Africa's lizards range in size from

Rock python

AFRIPICS

pinkie-length skinks to the 2-m long water monitor. One of the most familiar African lizards, often resident in hotel rooms, where it snaffles up insects attracted to the lights, is the house gecko, which is somewhat spectral in appearance due its almost transparent white skin, and has feet so adhesive it can run upside-down on a smooth ceiling. The agama family of garishly coloured lizards—blue, orange, purple and pink—is often associated with rocky habitats.

Gecko

163

Camouflage artist

Claude Hervé-Bazin

Chameleon *Chamaeleo*

As fast as lightening, the chameleon's tongue—as long as its body—shoots out, stuns the victim and glues it up. A fraction of a second later, the dreaded weapon is back in place, folded like an accordion at the back of the throat. With special 3-D vision, the chameleon can judge distances with precision; its eyes move independently, enabling it to see what's going on in front and behind. Contrary to legend, chameleons do not change colour for camouflage, but in response to their mood. Most species are green or brown in their normal state, but turn red or black when angry and white in the absence of light. Among the most striking of the 140 African chameleon species are those with horns (up to three), used in combat.

Nile crocodile
Crocodilus niloticus

The crocodile haunts most African rivers and lakes, and is often seen during the hottest hours of the day sunning on a sandbank. In the water, only its protruding nostrils, its eyes and part of the back are visible, like floating pieces of driftwood. The reptile lunges onto its prey and drags it thrashing underwater to drown, then leaves the body to tenderize beneath a rock or immersed tree trunk for a few days, since its teeth are not sharp enough to tear up fresh meat. A crocodile can go for six months without eating and lives up to 70 years. It lays eggs in the sand or mud of the river banks. The hatchlings measure 15 cm (6 in) at birth, growing into adults 6 m (20 ft) long.

Claude Hervé-Bazin

Jaw.

Birds

Kenya and Tanzania alone each boast in excess of 1,000 bird species and more than 1,700 have been recorded in eastern and southern Africa as a whole. Some of the more common and conspicuous savannah species are described below.

Fishy diet

Fish eagle *Haliaetus vocifer*

The most striking of more than a dozen African eagle species, the fish eagle is a familiar sight around the lakes and rivers, perched on its nest or on the topmost branches of a tall tree. It is easily recognized by its plumage: all the top of its body—head, neck and breast—is white, and the rest a brownish-black. It feeds on fish, which it skilfully skims from the lake surface, or on young flamingoes, leaving a nasty mess of pink feathers.

Ostrich *Struthio camelus*

Too bulky to fly, the ostrich has adapted to earthbound conditions by learning to run. With its long powerful legs, it can reach a speed of 70 kph (43 mph). It isn't exactly a featherweight: the full-grown male is about 2.4 m (8 ft) tall and weighs 140 kg. The ostrich lives in small groups dominated by one, polygamous male, with black plumage and white wings and tail feathers. The females are greyish-brown. They all

Claude Hervé-Bazin

Largest bird alive

lay eggs in the same nest, a large depression in the sand; there may be 40 eggs altogether, each weighing 2 kg! It's often said that the ostrich will eat anything. In fact, its diet consists of grass, fruit, insects and small mammals. It does, however, swallow a large quantity of sand. merely for digestive purposes.

Hornbills *Tockus spp*

These mostly black-and-white birds have large, curved beaks and some unusual habits. When nesting,

Behind closed doors…

the female walls herself up into the hollow of a tree, plastering over the entrance with mud which the male brings in pellets. Only a small slit is left for the male to pass in food. Once the eggs have hatched, the male provides for the whole family until the female can leave the nest. The chicks reseal the entrance and both parents continue to feed them until they are big enough to fend for themselves. The grey, yellow-billed 166 and red-billed hornbills, widespread in savannah habitats, are moderately large birds—about the size of a magpie—but they are dwarfed by forest species such as the trumpeter hornbill, which as its name suggests is also exceptionally noisy. More impressive still is the ground hornbill, a largely terrestrial savannah species that stands almost 1 m tall.

Flamingo

Phoeniconaias minor (Lesser flamingo)
Phoenicopterus ruber (Greater flamingo)

The greater flamingo is also found in the Mediterranean and the Caribbean, being twice as big as the lesser flamingo, by far the most abundant species. On the alkaline lakes of the East African Rift, the colonies can number up to 2 million birds, a spectacular sight. They feed on shrimp and microscopic algae, which give their feathers a pink tinge—dipping their heads under the water and scooping backwards with the head upside down. The bill is equipped with a filter that retains the food and strains out the water.

A flurry of pink

Claude Hervé-Bazin

Claude Hervé-Bazin

His royal highness

Snake charmer

Crowned crane
Balearica regulorum
With dark grey plumage and a golden fan-shaped crest, the crowned crane is one of the most handsome birds in Africa. It lives in pairs or small flocks near swamps, on lake shores and in grasslands. During the breeding season, they can be seen performing fascinating nuptial dances: face to face, the birds spread their wings, lift off suddenly into the air and let themselves fall, chase around on the ground and then start all over again.

Marabou stork
Leptoptilos crumeniferus
Bald, with a large, inflatable sack hanging from the base of its pink neck, the marabou stork is one of the ugliest birds in existence. It uses its long, strong beak to tear strips of flesh from decaying corpses. Its taste for carrion—or anything else of animal origin—has encouraged it to come closer to the towns where it feeds in rubbish tips. Like the other members of the stork family, the marabou is dumb: to make a noise it snaps its beak.

Secretary bird
Sagittarius serpentarius
Despite its long, thin legs, the bluish-grey secretary bird is a raptor, more closely related to eagles than to storks or cranes.

Garbage man

It seldom flies and is solitary, building nests of twigs in trees or bushes. It's often said that the name comes from its crest of feathers that look like quill pens stuck behind a clerk's ear, but in fact it is simply a mispronunciation of the Arabic name for the species. A fast runner, the bird preys on reptiles, especially snakes, stalking them through the grass and stunning them with its powerful, hooked beak and feet.

Highrises in the bush

Weavers *Ploceus spp*

Africa's many species of weaver are members of the passerine family. They are generally yellow in colour, or brown and black. The species known as the sociable weaver *(Philetairus socius)* builds round or bottle-shaped nests fixed to branches; one tree colony can consist of dozens of nests inhabited by up to 400 tenants. Using grass and other plant fibres, they weave their home according to a precise, complicated plan. The entry is almost always at the bottom.

Vultures

Among the more common of nine vulture species found in Africa are the hooded vulture *(Necrosyrtes monachus)* and the white backed vulture *(Gryps africanus)*. Most have similar features: an S-shaped neck, unfeathered head, large, hooked beak. And all vultures feed on carrion, which they spy from afar as they glide tirelessly over the savannah, taking advantage of rising thermals to stay high in the air without having to waste any effort. However, they are not very good at lifting off from the ground. Sometimes, when the bird has over-eaten (its gizzard can hold 6 kg of food), it just has to give up!

A morbid taste for bones

Claude Hervé-Bazin

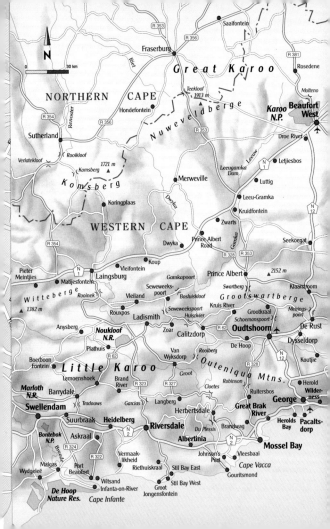

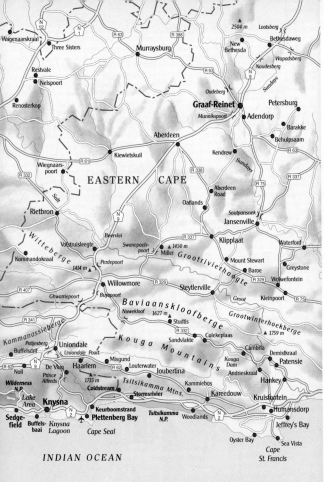

GARDEN ROUTE AND THE SOUTH